Mind RENOVATION

21 DAYS OF THOUGHT TRANSFORMATION

KRIS WHITE

DREAM TREE PRESS
DENTON, TEXAS

ISBN: 978-1-7320914-0-5 (TP) 978-1-7320914-1-2 (e)
Library of Congress Control Number: 2018902921
Published by: Dream Tree Press
P.O. Box 50808 Denton, Texas 76206
dreamtreepress.com

Cover design and interior sketches by Kendall Nicole Studios
Interior graphics courtesy of pixaby.com used with permission.

Dedicated to my Dad, Micheal C. Trammell.
Dreamer, builder and renovator.
Thank you for teaching me to honor hard work
and never to fear a toolbox.

You thought you were being made into a decent little cottage:
but He is building a palace.
He intends to come and live in it Himself.
——C. S. Lewis, Mere Christianity

. . . .

God is love. When we take up permanent residence in a life of love,
we live in God and God lives in us.
This way, love has the run of the house,
becomes at home and mature in us...
——1 John 4:17 The Message

Contents

ACKNOWLEDGMENTS

A special thank you to Sharron Jackson, who was my divinely designated cohort from the inception of this project. Your interest and ideas fueled my inspiration and provided the support I desperately needed to keep me on track. Everyone needs a friend like you. I'm thankful you're mine. Thank you for cheering me on to the finish line and for all your edits and professional help. I'm eternally grateful. To Pastor Perrianne Brownback, who has been my mentor for over 25 years, thank you for being my eternal sounding board who never wearies with my ideas.

To my family: To my firstborn, Kelsey Grace. Thank you for surprising me with a new computer. I'll never forget your sacrifice and love you showed me. Thank you for having faith in my words and being dedicated to our relationship from mom to daughter and now friend to friend. To my son, Cody, thank you for persistent chiding and encouragement to "lay some eggs" in my writing nook (the bird's nest), and my youngest daughter, Ashton Joy, for your prayers and strong words from God's heart to keep writing and not quit. Duane, my husband and best friend, thank you for always believing in my dreams and helping me transform my own mind with God's truth. Truth is greater than the facts. You are an echo of truth to my heart.

FOREWORD

God created our minds to serve the business of living and rally our ATTENTION to our INTENTIONS so that we can live a wide-open life in God's Spirit! The amazing brains on top of our heads are always busy logging data, processing emotion, distinguishing between alternatives and searching out patterns in experience. In short, they are miracles of lifelong learning! But, because we have functioned for periods of time without God's living truth on a subject—especially that of our identity—each of our minds has logged some bad data! My mind is amazing, but its ability to get stuck in disappointment, bitterness, misunderstanding or just natural thinking is also amazing—and limiting! And sometimes our minds, yet unaware of the Father's love for us, have even observed and chronicled patterns of failure and rejection that the enemy suggested to us. This is why each one of us must deal with the Scriptural directive in Romans 12:2 to be transformed by the renewing of our minds!

Mind renewal takes time and heart-focus, but you do not have to go it alone! The Holy Spirit will "coach" you through it, and as you cooperate, you will discover that your mind can serve your destiny rather than hinder it! There really is a flow possible—a place where our spirits and minds work together for the Kingdom of God! Kris White has written a book that opens the door to that flow. Her plan is not just a theoretical idea, but rather a practical travelogue to a new experience. What does true biblical mind renewal look like? Take a journey through Kris' daily applications of cleansing and begin to really *see!* Kris White introduces you to a whole new land of healthy living where that "thinking organ" atop your head can help and not hinder you!

As a close friend of Kris White's for many years, I have long known the thing that dawns quickly upon all her new audiences (whether they be "live" or via the printed page): Beneath that beautiful zest-for-life-and-creativity-laced exterior beats the heart of a true scholar! Kris absolutely knows how to make life fun, but never at the expense of faithfulness to the subtle nuances of biblical truth. Kris loves the Word of God. She processes life through her own exploits of family, travel and ministry, always filtering it through the glorious grid of God's revelation to us through Scripture! The product has a purity only the "incarnational drive" can give! I can promise you Kris has LIVED the anointed suggestions she makes to us here in these pages! She is now inviting you into her inner space and her desire is that you, too, would be well on your way to your God-adventure and fully able to take your mind right along with you!

Perrianne Brownback
Author and Pastor at The Abbey Church, Azle, Texas

INTRODUCTION
Your Mind is Prime Property!

"Imagine yourself as a living house. God comes in to rebuild that house. At first, perhaps, you can understand what He is doing. He is getting the drains right and stopping the leaks in the roof and so on; you knew that those jobs needed doing and so you are not surprised. But presently He starts knocking the house about in a way that hurts abominably and does not seem to make any sense. What on earth is He up to? The explanation is that He is building quite a different house from the one you thought of —throwing out a new wing here, putting on an extra floor there, running up towers, making courtyards. You thought you were being made into a decent little cottage: but He is building a palace. He intends to come and live in it Himself."— C. S. Lewis, Mere Christianity

Our house had just sold, and we were desperate to find a new one. I thought I had found my dream house with beautiful brand new hardwood floors, freshly painted walls, and never used appliances...but, the builder took another bid and we searched frantically to find another one. At the prompting of my daughter and the Holy Spirit, I thought, "I'm just going to drive through my favorite neighborhood again and see if maybe something's for sale that's not coming up on the internet search."

I turned the corner and couldn't believe my eyes. I rolled my car to a stop to get a closer look. The sign in front of the property read, "Coming Soon." It was a perfect location only five minutes from our church and had beautiful trees and a lake view in the backyard. After a frantic mission to retrieve my phone from my purse, I quickly called the agent's number. He hesitantly answered, "Ma'am, I don't want to show you this house yet. You've got to have EYES of POTENTIAL."

"Yes!" I replied. "Believe me, I have it! I can see potential!"

Reluctantly he agreed to let me see it. The hardwood floors were severely scratched, the cedar porch posts were rotting, the fixtures were outdated, and some kind of animal had clawed the baseboards. There was a hole in the master ceiling, cobwebs everywhere, and mounds of dog hair trapped inside both doors of the double oven (not sure how that happens). Destiny! I smiled and tried to contain my excitement. (I've learned excitement can increase value to salespersons.) "Yes, I see the potential, and I'd like to renovate it."

I am intrigued with the C. S. Lewis statement in *Mere Christianity* about how God Himself comes to rebuild the inner "living house" because "He intends to live there Himself." Yes, we are His temple. (1 Corinthians 6:19) We are the earthen vessel that houses the treasure. (2 Corinthians 4:7) We are "in Christ," and that has changed our potential and location (Ephesians 2:6)! In real estate everyone knows value is linked to location,

location, location! You can have a little dilapidated shanty worth a million dollars. Why? Because it's sitting on prime property with an ocean view.

The Bible encourages us in 2 Corinthians 3:18 to be transformed into His likeness with ever-increasing glory! He sees the POTENTIAL in you and knows your true value. Believe it or not there is a high appraisal on your life. In Christ your location is priceless! If this is true according to the Word of God, why does our thought life resemble a ransacked shack of panic, worry and fear? Your mind is not controlled by a slumlord forcing you to live in squalor. You have the "mind of Christ" and have access to the regenerating life of God. Those heavenly resources allow you the capital to RENOVATE those outdated and neglected rooms inside you! Romans 12:2 tells us to renew our thinking. This process renews the deteriorating ghetto of our negative thoughts into the creative charm of His original blueprint. You, my friend, are PRIME PROPERTY! There is a transformation with your name on it, but it's YOUR choice to hand the key over to the Master Builder. This isn't a DIY job.

This twenty-one day mind renovation is designed in three weeklong phases. The first phase, *Demolition*, helps us tear down faulty belief systems and remove debris from the past. The second phase, *Foundation*, guides us in rebuilding structures and patterns of truth.

The third phase, *Interior Furnishings*, helps us release creativity as we array our inner thoughts with His abundance. Each week offers a special tool for your toolbox of transformation.

Meditate on the daily scripture and ask the Holy Spirit to "enlighten your understanding" (Ephesians 1:18) to the toxic thoughts and habits of "stinking thinking." Write down areas where you find yourself worrying, or ruminating, over a negative thought, and turn it into a prayer. Then flip your self-talk pity party into a praise party of God's goodness. By repeating this action every day, you will form new habits that will clear the cobwebs of confusion, create new mindsets and literally change the chemistry of your brain.

God is the master Renovator! Invite Him into the front door of your mind. The Father wants to restore what the enemy has vandalized. So let the work (and the fun) begin! He's about to "flip" your mind, but He doesn't plan on selling—He's moving in to stay!

With love and eyes of potential,
Kris

You are God's field, God's building...Do you not know that you are God's temple and that God's Spirit dwells in you? — 1 Corinthians 3:9,16 (ESV)

WHY 21 DAYS?

For decades the magic number associated with breaking habits and creating new ones was twenty-one days. Dr. Maxwell Maltz's introduced this idea in the 1950s when he noticed plastic surgery patients took about twenty-one days to recognize their new face or to recover from feeling phantom limbs. In his popular book, *Psycho-Cybernetics,* he says, "...observed phenomena tend to show that it requires a minimum of twenty-one days for an old mental image to dissolve and a new one to jell." Self-help gurus jumped on the "21-Day" bandwagon and dubbed the enticing number the habit cure all. One word dropped from pop-psychology created a problem: *Minimum.* It takes a minimum of twenty-one days to see change.

Today scientists agree there is no exact formula for habit creation in the brain. Repetition is the key, but true transformation comes from a commitment to the process and a fervent desire to embrace the change. Let's not look at the next twenty-one days as a magic formula, but as a launching pad that sets your life in a new direction. It's intriguing how incubation for a baby chick takes twenty-one days. As you study this devotional for the next three weeks, I believe you'll not only experience the renovation of old thoughts, but an incubation of new ones beyond what you've dared to dream.

WHISTLE WHILE YOU WORK

One more thing before we start. Renovation is no walk in the park. It's hard work dislodging lies and rebuilding habits of healthy thinking. Since I was a child, my Dad whistled or sang while he worked. Believe me, he was no Sinatra, but his off-key melodies were infectious. They filled the air with a joyous optimism that eased the burden of the task and somehow made the manual labor seem fun. He'd sing his favorite songs over and over until they got stuck in your mind like a broken record. If I close my eyes and listen now, I can still hear his songs.

As we journey through the next twenty-one days, I pray you hear your heavenly Father's whistle over you. It's described for us in Zephaniah 3:17.

> For the Lord your God is living among you. He is a mighty savior. He will take delight in you with gladness. With his love, he will calm all your fears. He will rejoice over you with joyful songs.
> — Zephaniah 3:17-18 NLT —

He's singing a joyous song over you, over every anxious thought, over every racing question. Can you hear Him? He's singing a song of freedom. It's your victory song inspired by His enduring love for you. Keep listening. Focus into His voice. Before long you'll start whistling along, and I pray His song gets really stuck in your head!

Phase 1: DEMOLITION

TEARING DOWN FAULTY BELIEF SYSTEMS AND REMOVING DEBRIS FROM THE PAST

We use our powerful God-tools for smashing warped philosophies, tearing down barriers erected against the truth of God, fitting every loose thought and emotion and impulse into the structure of life shaped by Christ.
- 2 Corinthians 10:5 The Message

If you've ever watched any home renovation show, then you know how exciting demo day is! Well...**IT'S DEMO DAY!** (The crowd goes wild!) People go crazy swinging sledgehammers and shattering outdated bathroom fixtures in a cloud of glorious dust. All caution is thrown to the wind in an attempt to remove the old and prepare a fresh palette for the new.

Demolition is not for the faint of heart. It requires crazy courage and a vision for the future. That promise inspires us to put on the work boots, roll up our sleeves and prepare for a lot of mess and unexpected surprises.

Demolition = the act of completely destroying or demolishing in order to use for something else; to tear down, break to pieces, do away with; to utterly defeat; act of breaking apart especially with explosives.

Demolition confirms the conclusion. The past purpose has culminated, and it must be cleared for something new to replace it. We cannot lay new fresh carpet on top of the old dingy red shag and expect a change. It's got to be rolled up and removed. Just imagine trying to hang crisp new wallpaper over decaying moldy walls. The mold or any other rotten thing has to be disposed of, or as 2 Corinthians 10:5 instructs, "taken into captivity." Take heart. Sometimes things "look" worse before they get better. You may be tempted to regret your endeavor. True renovation cannot happen without removal of the outdated and broken things that can't serve your present purpose. God's anointing on the prophet Jeremiah was not only to build up but also to tear down.

"See, I have this day set you over the nations and over the kingdoms, to root out and pull down, to destroy and throw down, to build and to plant." — Jeremiah 1:10 (NKJV)

Israel adopted many carnal mindsets and attitudes that needed to be uprooted before the promise of their deliverance manifested. Jeremiah implored them, *"...wash your heart from wickedness, that you may be saved. How long shall your evil thoughts lodge with you?"* (Jeremiah 4:14 NKJV)

It's time to dislodge those thoughts! There's a divine anointing and empowering to tear down those thoughts that aren't aligned with God's nature. Some attitudes are removed with repentance and some mindsets only move with the explosive power of praise and agreement of God's truth.

What things must be broken down and uprooted in your thinking? What thoughts need to be tossed into the dumpster? What thoughts can be recycled and redeemed when tweaked and repositioned into a different light? Are you ready? IT'S DEMO WEEK!

TAKE UP YOUR TOOL: AGREEMENT

A real renovator has a full toolbox and knows how to use them. Phase One offers the tool of AGREEMENT, which is crucial to tearing down old mindsets and building on truth. Agreeing with God's thoughts and who He has made us in Christ is essential to any thought freedom. The question is, will you agree with the arguments or acknowledge the truth?

Agreement = a formal decision about future action that is made by two or more, a joint decision that a particular course of action should be taken, having the same opinion. (Collins Dictionary)

"The tools of our trade aren't for marketing or manipulation, but they are for demolishing that entire massively corrupt culture. We use our powerful God-tools for smashing warped philosophies, tearing down barriers erected against the truth of God, fitting every loose thought and emotion and impulse into the structure of life shaped by Christ. Our tools are ready at hand for clearing the ground of every obstruction and building lives of obedience into maturity."
—2 Corinthians 10:4-6 (The Message)

 Agreement is like a hammer that tears down old lies and fixes truth in place. It is internally processed then verbally pronounced.

TAKE ACTION:

Throughout the day make a conscience effort to notice your thoughts. At the end of each day journal what your

Celebrate little things

thoughts drifted toward and how they affected your feelings and your choices. Ask yourself if the thought agrees with God's truth or the enemy's lies. (John 10:10)

"I think God's thoughts after him" — Johannes Kepler

STOP AND REGAIN CONTROL OF YOUR THOUGHTS:

what you thought of the most each day

S. = Stop, don't act immediately.

T. = Take a minute to breathe.

O. = Observe what your thoughts are. Are they true? How are they affecting your emotions and your behavior?

give more compliments

P. = Pray about what you're thinking and ask God for His perspective. Pull back from the immediate circumstance and look at the big picture. **Will this matter in 10 minutes, 10 months or 10 years?**

your mindset = my mindset

to see me through your eyes

Trust in him, give him all of it.

Think before

Notice thoughts toxic?

Changing your mindset

DAY 1: WHO'S SQUATTING IN YOUR HEAD?

RENOVATING THOUGHT: IT'S MY RESPONSIBILITY TO MANAGE THE PROPERTY IN MY MIND.

"For who has known the mind and purposes of the Lord, so as to instruct Him? But we have the mind of Christ [to be guided by His thoughts and purposes]."—1 Corinthians 2:16 (AMP)

The first step in renovation is confirming ownership. No remodel or restoration can begin without the validation of who owns the property; but also importantly, who has possession of the property! Both of these things are vital. You may own the title to a property, but if others are squatting in it, they must be evicted before renovation can begin.

not to second guess myself

SQUATTER'S RIGHTS

It is astounding how many times squatters derail housing renovations. The *Los Angeles Times* reported the story of a man who inherited his father's southern California townhouse free and clear of any mortgage. The man lived five hours away so he would only come from time to time to get mail and check on things. Over time his diligence to oversee it waned, and he left it to sit vacant and unattended. Unbeknownst to him, squatters moved in, changed the locks and even attended HOA (Home Owner Association) meetings where they voted on things for the community! [1] Squatter's rights are a significant issue in many places, especially California. The laws originated in England when hundreds of years ago, abandoned property could be taken over by people willing to work the land. The key to revoking these squatter's rights, or "adverse possession" as termed legally, is for the property owner to press a claim within the time frame declared by the state's law. Or in other words, property owners must be diligent to watch over their property and immediately take action if a freeloader tries to move in! Squatters' rights grow stronger with every day they're allowed to remain.

PRESS YOUR CLAIM

As a believer in Christ, you are a new creation and all ownership to your life has been transferred to the kingdom of heaven. Jesus paid the price for your salvation on the cross. The title of your life is in His hands free and clear, but He's entrusted stewardship over to you. You have authority and the responsibility to manage the property of your soul (mind, will and emotions). The only problem is that you have some squatters that are claiming "adverse possession" of your mind. Thoughts of fear, doubt, depression and insecurity have taken up possession and tried to change the locks on you. These rogue thoughts even think their votes count in the HOA of your destiny! Well, it's time to dispossess them and reclaim your property!

We are called to imitate Jesus and reveal His nature on the earth, so our minds are called to look like His. We are called to think God's thoughts! 1 Corinthians 2:16 says, "we have the mind of Christ." The Greek word for "have" is *echo*.

Isn't that wonderful! We are called and empowered to echo the mind of Christ. His mind met fear with faith. His mind met lack with heaven's resource. His mind met offense with forgiveness. Christ has given us the power to echo His heavenly mindset as we start to reclaim our minds for His kingdom. In his book, *The Heart: The Key to Everything in the Christian Life*, Tim Rowe beautifully states, "the only way we win the battle of our thinking is to surrender it to him. He purchased us with the price of his precious blood and our thought life is now his possession. Give him what is rightfully his! We have no right to be the masters of our thinking any longer. Jesus Christ wants to take up residence in our thinking and be the Captain, the Savior, the Mighty One and the Lord of all the thoughts that mold and fashion our hearts." [2]

Before renovation begins, we must be clear about ownership and possession. <u>You can have control over your thoughts instead of your thoughts controlling you!</u> Get in there and show them who's boss! Reclaim your mind. Evict those squatting thoughts you've let live rent free in your head and revoke their HOA votes.

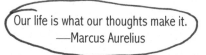

Our life is what our thoughts make it.
—Marcus Aurelius

RETHINK:

⇒ Who or what has been managing your thought property?

⇒ Do your thoughts and feelings control you, or do you control them?

⇒ If Jesus came to check up on how you've been stewarding the property He paid to give you, how would your evaluation be? (Read the Parable of the Talents in Matthew 25:14-30 for a refresher on Jesus' thoughts of stewardship.)

⇒ What specific thoughts have been squatting in your "thought house" that need eviction?

⇒ Does your mind look like it's saved? Does it reflect the thoughts of God?

RENOVATION PRAYER:

Father, in the name of Jesus, I reclaim my mind for you. I give ownership of my heart and mind fully to you and accept the responsibility you gave me to steward them. I take authority over my thoughts and declare, "I have the mind of Christ." Jesus, you died to bring salvation and healing to my mind; I receive this healing now. I pray my thoughts would echo your thoughts. I declare that thoughts of _____
(fill in the blank for the squatting thoughts trying to control your mind) have no right to stay and live rent free in my head. I receive the power to change *and reclaim my role and responsibility in this mind* renovation. *Thank you, Lord, for your grace and strength. In the powerful name of Jesus, amen.*

DEMOLITION DUMP:
What thoughts need to be dumped out and NOT allowed back?

believing I'm not enough for others

AGREEMENT: *What thought focuses your agreement to God's truth today?*

DAY 2: IT'S THE THOUGHT THAT COUNTS

RENOVATING THOUGHT: MY THOUGHTS SHAPE MY LIFE.

"For as he thinks in his heart, so is he." —*Proverbs 23:7a (AMP)*

We think of the phrase "it's the thought that counts" when someone gives us a handful of dandelions or a homemade potholder, but the truth of this statement far exceeds the context of a simple gift. **Your thoughts count every second and are shaping your life!** Scientists agree the average person thinks between 50,000 and 80,000 thoughts per day. These thoughts determine the direction of a person's life.

> "Sow a thought, reap an action. Sow an action, reap a habit, Sow a habit, reap a character. Sow a character, reap a destiny."
> —Author Unknown

NETWORKING NEURONS

Let's give a round of applause to our Creator. Our brains are the most complicated objects in the universe. They are composed of about 100 billion neurons networked by trillions of connections called synapses, which transmit up to 1,000 signals per second.[1]

Neurons that fire together, wire together. Hebb's Law

Until the last thirty years, scientists considered no significant connection between our mind and our physical brain. But new research proves what many Christians believed for centuries: there is a physical link between our minds and our body.

Thoughts are electronic impulses feeding our brains with positive or negative energy. These impulses affect the body's chemistry and hormones as well as mental wellbeing. You might think your thoughts are secret and harmless, but they are shaping your brain and determining your genetic readout.

A TALE OF TWO TREES

Dr. Caroline Leaf, a South African neuroscientist, along with others in her field, describes the neurons in the brain as trees. As we think toxic negative thoughts, the neurons branch out—limb after limb creating dead-looking trees. The more we develop these negative thoughts, the faster these trees turn into forests!

Your thoughts are actually shaping your brain.

As we think healthy thoughts, we grow fruitful branches. This fascinating fact reminds us of the promise in Psalm 1:3, *"He shall be like a tree, planted by the rivers of water, that brings forth its fruit in its season, whose leaf also shall not wither, and whatever he does shall prosper."* *(NKJV)* This is God's dream for your mind—to become like a fruitful orchard. Your thoughts, whether toxic or healthy, will become the scaffolding to the architecture of your life.

Brain changes

mind makes you strong

Believe in yourself

water helps it grow

mind - God

roots deep

your thoughts shape you

Dr. Leaf teaches that thoughts actually have the power to affect our DNA.

"We may have a fixed set of genes in our chromosomes, but which of those genes is active ... has a great deal to do with how we think and process our subjective experiences, i.e. our reactions... We are constantly reacting to the circumstances and events of this life and as this cycle goes on, our brains become shaped in a process that will either be in a positive direction or a negative direction. So it is the quality of our thinking and choices, our reactions, which determine our brain architecture." [2]

In his book, *Tree of the Brain, Roots of the Mind*, Giorgio Ascoli makes many provocative claims about the relationship between the mind and the brain. He says, "If each nerve cell enlarged a thousand fold looks like a tree, then a small region of the nervous system at the same magnified scale resembles a gigantic, fantastic forest." Ascoli proposes some of the most intriguing mysteries of the mind can be solved using the basic architectural principles of the brain.[3] And what shapes that architecture? Our thoughts! That's why Paul encourages us in Romans 12:2 to renew our minds. It rebuilds our life!

Your thoughts are the scaffolding that shapes the
architecture of your life.

Jesus told others many times in the New Testament that He knew their thoughts or hearts. In Matthew 5 He emphasized the importance of our inner thought life. He shocked many in the crowd by saying, "I tell you that anyone who looks at a woman lustfully has already committed adultery with her in his heart." (Matthew 5:27 NIV) The Greek word for "heart" here is the word *kardia*, which means "the center and seat of spiritual life, the soul or mind." [4] Our mind (reasoning center) makes up a significant part of our soul (mind, will and emotions). God looks through the outside walls of success or failure, religion or rebellion, ability or inadequacy into the HEART.

"But the LORD said to Samuel, do not consider his appearance or his height, for I have rejected him. The LORD does not look at the things people look at. People look at the outward appearance, but the LORD looks at the heart." — 1 Samuel 16:7 (NIV)

If we're called to live inside out, with His Spirit residing in us, our thoughts create the architecture of our heart and in turn direct our life.

take control

Your mind matters. On Day Two of Demolition Week, take inventory of your thought life. The good, the bad and the ugly. Let's tear down any forests of toxic thoughts that have shaped your life and endeavor to plant healthy thoughts that yield a fruitful orchard.

"You shall love the Lord...with all your mind."
— *Matthew 22:37 (NIV)*

RETHINK:

⇒ If your day's thoughts were played like a feature 3D presentation on a high-definition cinema screen, what impact would it have on people?

⇒ What's the impact on you now?

⇒ What genre and rating would have to be placed on it? (How much is not suitable for children? Or you as a child of God?)

⇒ What are some feelings you struggle with? Can you see toxic trees of thought that feed that feeling?

⇒ For further study, read about how "brain trees" or dendrites are formed.

⇒ Write down five thoughts you want to dwell on in your mind today that reflect God's truth. How can you SERVE and LOVE the Lord with your mind? (Matthew 22:37)

RENOVATION PRAYER

Father, search me and show me destructive thought patterns that do not agree with Your Word. I repent of any toxic thoughts influencing my body's health in a negative way. I pray for healing and restoration for any negative patterns or "trees" I have allowed to form in my mind. Help me think the thoughts today that lead me into my destiny. I pray you would rewire my toxic thoughts into healthy thoughts of a fruitful, abundant life. In Jesus' name, amen.

DEMOLITION DUMP:
What thoughts need to be dumped out and NOT allowed back?

I overthink things and not enough

AGREEMENT: *What thought focuses your agreement to God's truth today?*

Take control of your life, plan things out. Don't wait for others to do things for you or remind you.

DAY 3: BREAKING THROUGH BARRIERS

RENOVATING THOUGHT: I TAKE EVERY THOUGHT CAPTIVE TO THE OBEDIENCE OF CHRIST.

"We use our powerful God-tools for smashing warped philosophies, tearing down barriers erected against the truth of God, fitting every loose thought and emotion and impulse into the structure of life shaped by Christ. Our tools are ready at hand for clearing the ground of every obstruction and building lives of obedience into maturity."
—2 Corinthians 10:5-6 (The Message)

It's time to clear out everything that's not God's original design. Some of us just need to remove a few limiting opinions, like popping up old tiles in the kitchen, but some of us need a wrecking ball to break through the barriers in our minds!

Do you have your clipboard ready? This is our demolition list of items that must go. I like how remodeling professionals walk into the house with a can of red spray paint and mark a big X on the items for removal. Once it's marked, it can't negotiate its way back. Today, let's mark those things that must be removed from your thoughts!

My husband, Duane White, shares in his book, *Huperman*, about the backwards progression of 2 Corinthians 10:4-5 from "high things" to "arguments or imaginations" to "strongholds:"

The weapons we fight with are not the weapons of the world. On the contrary, they have divine power to demolish **strongholds**. *We demolish* **arguments** *and every* **pretension** *that sets itself up against the knowledge of God, and we take captive every thought to make it obedient to Christ. (NIV, emphasis added)*

This progression reveals barriers to a renovated mind that must be demolished.

DEMO LIST:

1. High Things (pretensions or opinions) that exalt itself against the knowledge of God *(Hypsōma: thing elevated, height, barrier / an evil spirit or principality.)* [1]

The enemy begins with a single, ambiguous thought. It seems harmless at first, but if not captured and evicted, like the rogue squatter, this thought gathers friends and links together to raise a barrier against God's truth. For example, a thought floats into Derek's mind that God doesn't love him as much as his brother who just got married and received a great promotion at work. Derek has a choice to either take this thought captive and exalt God's truth over it, or to let it promote itself in his mind as higher than God's opinion. If he lets it stay and settle, it searches for more pretensions that agree with it. These pretensions band together to form a "high thing" or "barrier of thought in the mind" that exalts itself "above the knowledge of what God says about the situation or the truth." [2]

2. Argument or Vain Imagination *(Logismos: a reckoning, computation, reasonings that bring a verdict.[3])*

As these opinions grow they band together to form arguments, or "vain imaginations". (KJV) These false imaginations can be thought of as "image-nations," or complete nations, of faulty thought patterns, mindsets and ways of seeing things. Continuing our example, Derek's mind has gathered a lot of other pretensions of why God doesn't love him. His acceptance of that original lie caused him to look for other supporting evidence. His mom sided with this brother in a discussion, his car broke down and a girl turned him down for a date. Now these arguments have demanded the verdict over his life that nothing good will ever happen to him because he's not loved. The devil is successfully crafting thought patterns and filters of constant insecurity and victimization.

bad things happen

These walls lead to the next demolition item...

3. Strongholds *(Ochyrōma: a castle, stronghold, fortress, fastness; anything on which one relies.[4])*

The high things that formed arguments have now leagued together to form a stronghold. Put simply, a stronghold is anything that has a strong hold on your mind, pulling it away from God. A stronghold pulls your attention and requires you to trust and rely on it above God's promise. Addiction, bitterness, insecurity, poverty and fear can all become strongholds that imprison us. They are the devil's strategy to "steal, kill and destroy" us. (John 10:10) It all started with one little thought we didn't take captive.

negative thoughts   worry   decisions

What consumes your thoughts, controls your life.

Stress

Back to our story of Derek, as he continued to agree with the arguments, they fortified a stronghold, like a prison, around his mind. Now Derek has secluded himself from others, doubts God exists and resigned to a life of misery. Do you even remember the original opinion that formed the first brick in his stronghold?

A stronghold is anything pretending to be bigger than God.
— Beth Moore

HOW DO WE DEMOLISH STRONGHOLDS?

Our weapons or "God-tools" are mighty to demolish and pull down these warped walls. The Greek word for "pulling down" is *kathairesis*, which means "to lower."[5] To demo these strongholds, we must "lower them" in our opinion and exalt God's truth over the false argument. Tim Rowe writes, "Idolatry is at the heart of every stronghold."[6] The devil wants you to worship his thoughts (or lies) over God's. A stronghold is redirected worship! We start to break through these walls when we

REVEAL them for what they are, REMOVE the lies and false verdicts and REPLACE them with truth.

Then you will know the truth, and the truth will set you free.
— John 8:32 (NIV)

RETHINK:

⇒ What argument or vain imagination has been wearing you down and talking you out of victory?

⇒ What stronghold is causing you to rely on it instead of the strength of God? Can you locate the first "high thing" that began the fortress?

⇒ What is your DEMO Day plan? Are there physical things you need to trash (or give away) as a symbol of your freedom?

Comparing myself

⇒ What can you do physically to block access to the old strongholds?

⇒ How can you adopt the "Reveal, Remove and Replace" habit in your life?

RENOVATION PRAYER

In the name of Jesus, I tear down every stronghold, argument or high thing that's been built in my thinking. I exalt the knowledge of Jesus as my Lord and Savior over every lie and declare that the TRUTH will make me free. I receive freedom from comparison *(insert your own). I declare I am set free from the power of any evil thoughts or spirits by the blood and power of Jesus. Father, forgive me for exalting any lie or argument from the enemy over your truth. I will worship you, and I will agree with your thoughts and truths. I break any agreements or vows I have made with these thoughts. Lord, demolish them out of my life. I denounce any unclean spirit I may have opened myself up to. I declare Jesus is my Savior, and I give my life to Him. Holy Spirit, empower me to take them captive when they try to reason their way back into my mind. I am free! In the powerful name of Jesus, it is finished.*

DEMOLITION DUMP:
What thoughts need to be dumped out and NOT allowed back?

I am my own person and I
will get through it.

AGREEMENT: *What thought focuses your agreement to God's truth today?*

He has a plan I need to
put trust in him to know it wont
always be bad and stressful and
I will find my place.

DAY 4: GET YOUR MIND OUT OF THE GUTTER

RENOVATING THOUGHT: THE BLOOD OF JESUS CLEANSES OUR MIND OF PAST SIN, MEMORIES AND HURTS.

But if we walk in the light, as he is in the light, we have fellowship with one another, and the blood of Jesus his Son cleanses us from all sin.
—*1 John 1:7 (NKJV)*

Surprisingly, the highest remodeling costs are often trash removal and dumpster rentals! Many times contractors walk into projects where the tenants deserted the property and left behind heaps of garbage. Imagine this scene: old, putrid milk on the counter, maggot-infested food scraps in the sink, heaps of sweaty, stained clothing in every corner and rancid human waste in the bathrooms. Can you see and *smell* the picture?

Don't wallow on bad things

29

Many things can add to garbage thoughts in our minds. Maybe you've had trash thoughts thrown at you since childhood, like how stupid, ugly and worthless you are. Maybe there's trash in your thoughts from the memories of past sins. Those thoughts can pile up fast and start to stink. Many refer to this as "stinking thinking." Just like the reno garbage needs to be purged, so does your mind!

"I'm baptizing you here in the river, turning your old life in for a kingdom life. The real action comes next: The main character in this drama—compared to him I'm a mere stagehand—will ignite the kingdom life within you, a fire within you, the Holy Spirit within you, changing you from the inside out. He's going to clean house—make a clean sweep of your lives. He'll place everything true in its proper place before God; everything false he'll put out with the trash to be burned."
— Matthew 3:11-12 The Message

THOUGHTS FROM A ROOF

How could such a great leader make such a big mistake? King David, a man after God's own heart, let his own thought life pile up with sins of lust. Strolling on the roof of the palace after a nap, he saw her bathing, beautiful Bathsheba. We cannot control what thoughts run across the ticker tape of our minds, but we do control if we allow them to remain, take root and become action.

David could have taken that thought captive. Instead, it remained and turned into acts of adultery. Soon David's mind raced with a growing web of guilt and lies,

we can control what we do or for the better

raise a higher standard

peace

culminating in his sending Bathsheba's husband to the front lines to be killed. (2 Samuel 11) We can imagine David's internal conversation as a war zone between darkness and light. The devil prodding him toward sin in one second and turning with pointed finger to condemn and shame him the next; the Holy Spirit drawing him back to God's purposes with whispers of wisdom and truth.

"The thing David had done displeased the Lord." (2 Samuel 11:27 NIV) Yet as David humbled himself, God's power washed his heart and mind. David tells us about this beautiful cleansing in Psalm 51.

Please God + yourself not just others.

Have mercy on me, O God, according to your unfailing love; according to your great compassion blot out my transgressions. Wash away all my iniquity and cleanse me from my sin. — Psalms 51:1 (NIV)

can't deney

We have all thought ugly, sinful thoughts. (Romans 3:23) These thoughts either lead to regrettable actions like David's, or affect us like Bathsheba-making us the victim of someone's sinful choices. The sin cycle will continue until it is power washed and redeemed by the blood of Jesus.

Peace, perfect peace, in this dark world of sin?
The Blood of Jesus whispers peace within.
—Sir Ahmed Salman Rushdie

find it

So around yourself with people who build you up.

THERE IS POWER IN THE BLOOD OF JESUS!

"But now in Christ Jesus you who once were far off have been brought nearby the blood of Christ." — Ephesians 2:13 (NKJV)

"...for this is my blood of the covenant, which is poured out for many for the forgiveness of sins." — Matthew 26:28 (NIV)

Wherever you are right now, can you thank God for sending Jesus to cleanse you of every evil, harassing thought? What is that sin that you are ashamed to think of? That thing the enemy holds over you as blackmail, condemning you if you try to move past it. Is it hiding in the closet buried under heaps of rubbish? Can you see Jesus walking into the room, taking the weight of that sin and carrying it out to the dumpster?

notice his presence

Only the blood of Jesus can cleanse us, yet if we withhold ourselves from that blood, we will be unclean forever. —A.W. Tozer

RENOVATION PRAYER

Jesus, I repent for all the evil thoughts I have hidden and harbored. I thank you that you gave your perfect life and your perfect mind for me to be free. You shed your blood for me on the cross. You paid the price for me to be cleansed, purified, freed and released from all these thoughts of guilt. I plead the blood of Jesus over my mind. Wash every thought. Create in me a pure heart and mind. In Your name, Jesus, amen.

He promises to
wash it all away.

Become a new
creation

Picture Jesus' blood pouring over every thought throughout your entire life. Whenever the enemy tries to bring something back up, shout, "No, that's covered in the blood!" *He removes it all*

Now you've dealt with your sin, but what about the thoughts that haunt you from other people's sin? There is no sin —yours or the effects of someone else's —that Jesus' blood cannot purify. This time think about the incident that caused you pain. Maybe it was someone else's "gutter thoughts" that have made YOU feel dirty! You can be cleansed.

Let's pray again: *Jesus, thank You for Your sacrifice on the cross that gave me freedom from the sins of others. I pray your blood would come right now and cleanse my mind from the terror of every event that haunts my mind. Take out the years of trash that has piled up from other people's bad choices. I choose to forgive them now, as you have forgiven me. In Your name, Jesus, amen.*

Now picture the blood of Jesus washing over every injustice and wrong made against you from before you were born to today!

It's in the past, let it go, he has it.

RETHINK:

⇒ Journal about what God did in your mind when you prayed the renovation prayers. Which had a tighter grip on you—the thought of *your* sins or someone *else's*?

⇒ Write out some scriptures on the power of the blood of Jesus. Read Hebrews 9 and make notes on the things that stand out to you.

⇒ Find a song about the blood of Jesus, such as "Nothing but the Blood", and sing it to remind yourself of what God's done for you.

DEMOLITION DUMP:
What thoughts need to be dumped out and NOT allowed back?

The guilt and thoughts, self doubts
Grudges I have.

AGREEMENT: *What thought focuses your agreement to God's truth today?*

let it all go and live as
a new person, Know he will
Slowly take it all away.

DAY 5: BRAINWASHED

RENOVATING THOUGHT: MEDITATING ON THE WORD OF GOD CLEANSES MY MIND.

"...Christ loved the church and gave himself up for her to make her holy, cleansing her by the washing with water through the word..."
— *Ephesians 5:25-26 (NIV)*

Remember the old-fashioned punishment of washing your mouth out with soap? Wouldn't it be great if fixing our words was as easy as washing our tongues! We know our words flow from what's in our hearts and minds, so perhaps what we truly need isn't a tongue wash but a mind wash!

The Apostle Paul teaches in Ephesians 5:26 that God's Word does just that — it washes our minds! But just how does this happen? It's a lot more than rubbing a Bible on our head like a paperback loofa. If the blood of Jesus can wash away our sin, how can we keep our minds clean?

MIND MEDITATION

Scripture reveals God's thoughts, and His thoughts become a part of our thoughts when we meditate on the scriptures. Meditation is the process of mulling something over in your mind and mouth. Sadly, in our culture this word conjures up New Age images of people sitting in the lotus position muttering, "OHMMMMM." Meditation originated long before yoga mats. It was God's idea. He created our minds to work this way, processing and learning with reflection and repetition.

Cause me to understand the way of your precepts, that I may meditate on your wonderful deeds. — Psalms 119:27 (NIV)

Eastern mystics have tried to hijack this ancient scriptural principle by encouraging students to empty their minds, but God's word always encourages us to DIRECT our minds. Remember, we have the mind of Christ. Never open your mind up to any meditations, teachings, or spirits that don't submit to the obedience of Jesus Christ. This can be very dangerous and open you up to demonic spirits. We are one with Christ, not the universe. The only spirit we want to dwell in our minds is the Holy Spirit.

find things
about yourself
new clean things

NEW OPERATING SYSTEM

When a computer is upgraded, it requires a new operating system. When we receive Jesus and give our lives to Him, we need a new operating system for our soul. That system is only downloaded by renewing our minds with God's word. Just as God spoke and created the world we see, His written word is powerful to create a new world in us!

An unread Bible is like food that is refused, an unopened love letter, a buried sword, a road map not studied, a gold mine not worked.
—Irving L. Jensen [1]

Wash my thoughts with your Word.

positive things, true

things others see we dont about ourselves

WHY SHOULD WE MEMORIZE SCRIPTURE?

It may seem like an old-fashioned thing to do, but memorizing scripture and knowing God's truth transforms and renews our minds. Dennis Lennon writes, "*What the heart knows by heart, the heart really knows.*"

Do what I say and you'll live well. My teaching is as precious as your eyesight—guard it! Write it out on the back of your hands; etch it on the chambers of your heart. — Proverbs 7:2 (The Message)

MEMORIZING GOD'S WORD:

✓ Enables us to know God's truth and promise over us. Reciting His Word changes our perspective and reminds us how God sees things. We can flip worry into a declaration of His Word.

✓ Helps us meditate on and cultivate God's truth in us. When we know the Word we can easily mull it over in our minds. Reciting the Word cleanses our mind and creates healthy pathways in our brain.

✓ Gives us words to pray in faith. When we don't know what to pray, we pray His promises. Faith comes where the will of God is known. Praying His Word is praying His will.

✓ Releases wisdom to make right choices: We hide His Word in our hearts so that we will not sin against His ways. (Psalm 119:11)

✓ Comforts us and helps us encourage others: "Remember your promise to me; it is my only hope. Your promise revives me; it comforts me in all my troubles." (Psalm 119:49-50 NLT)

✓ Fights our battles in the spirit. We fight the enemy with the sword of the Spirit — the Word of God. (Ephesians 6:17) Jesus answered the devil's temptations in the wilderness with the Word. It is a double-edged sword, used for offense and defense. (Hebrews 4:12) Offensively the Word pulls down strongholds and breaks the power of the enemy. On the defense, the Scriptures defend the faith and give witness of its truth to others.

I'LL TAKE THE SWORD

On a family trip to Edinburgh, Scotland while we were serving as missionaries in the UK, we visited a wool shop. I could not pass up a photo opportunity to don Scottish kilts and tartans and honor my Scottish ancestry. After dressing in our plaid Celtic attire, the photographer arranged the family for the photo. My youngest daughter, Ashton, who was about five years old at the time, was positioned in the front of the family and presented with a bouquet of heather. She looked up at the photographer and announced, "Hey Mister, I want the sword!" She refused to smile for the picture until she was given a sword that was almost as tall as she was.

Let the cry of our hearts be, "I want my sword!" There is authority and power in the inspired, God-breathed Word of God! It will wash our minds and keep them in purity.

RETHINK:

⇒ What priority do you put on reading and studying the Bible?

⇒ What is your attitude toward memorizing scripture? Which reasons leapt out to you?

⇒ In which areas does your brain need to be washed (lust, fear, jealousy, anger)? Find scriptures to wash your mind with the Word. Write them on note cards and place them where you will see them often.

⇒ Read Psalm 119. Highlight key verses. Journal your insights into loving His commands.

⇒ Study the S.O.A.P. approach to meditating on a scripture. (Consider adding a "Y" to make it S.O.A.P.Y. The Y is for "Yes!"

Write your declaration of faith in agreement with God's promise.) See Appendix.

RENOVATION PRAYER

Father, I ask you to wash my mind with your Word. Give me a desire to know it and hide it in my heart so that I will not sin against you. Let your Word create a new world in me and renew my thoughts. Let your Word be a light to my path and guide me into truth. Enlarge my capacity to understand and remember your Word. Teach me to use the sword of the Spirit as a weapon of victory in my life. In Jesus name, amen.

DEMOLITION DUMP:

What thoughts need to be dumped out and NOT allowed back?

I am unclean I let sin control me.

AGREEMENT: *What thought focuses your agreement to God's truth today?*

I can clean myself with Christ

DAY 6: RENEW YOUR ATTITUDE

RENOVATION THOUGHT: ATTITUDE DETERMINES ALTITUDE, AND I HAVE THE POWER TO RENEW IT.

You were taught, with regard to your former way of life, to put off your old self, which is being corrupted by its deceitful desires; to be made new in the attitude of your minds; and to put on the new self, created to be like God in true righteousness and holiness. —Ephesians 4:22-23 (NIV)

I nevitably on home renovation shows, the homeowner must decide to recycle it, reuse it or repurpose it. The designer negotiates for the removal of tattered recliners, outdated appliances and clashing wall colors. But change is scary, and it's hard to part with what's familiar and comfortable. "You're going to love it! It will be worth it," the professional encourages. "Just trust me." Maybe we've heard whispers of this before.

A NEW DAY REQUIRES A NEW ATTITUDE

The Bible discussed this phenomenon when it taught about putting new wine in old wineskins.

Then Jesus gave them this illustration: "No one tears a piece of cloth from a new garment and uses it to patch an old garment. For then the new garment would be ruined, and the new patch wouldn't even match the old garment. And no one puts new wine into old wineskins. For the new wine would burst the wineskins, spilling the wine and ruining the skins. New wine must be stored in new wineskins. But no one who drinks the old wine seems to want the new wine. 'The old is just fine,' they say.
— *Luke 5:36-39 (NLT)*

A new day requires a new attitude! Zig Ziglar shared many times how "attitude, not aptitude, determines altitude." The word "attitude" comes from the Latin word for "posture" or "position." Your attitude is your stance or position on what's going on in your life. Attitude affects our climate internally and externally. Joyce Meyer writes, "Attitude is your thought life turned inside out." If you've ever dealt with someone with a bad attitude, you know the effect they can have on everyone in the room.

Attitude is your thought life turned inside out.
— Joyce Meyer

In Ephesians 4, we are instructed not to live in futile thinking caused by darkness in understanding and hard hearts toward God. This futile thinking asks, "How does this affect me and make me feel?" (Me-centered). In contrast, we are to reflect our new "position in Christ" (Galatians 2:20). We are to ask, "How can this reveal Christ and build the Kingdom of God?" (Christ-centered). This reborn position requires a new attitude!

You were taught, with regard to your former way of life, to put off your old self, which is being corrupted by its deceitful desires; to be made new in the attitude of your minds; and to put on the new self, created to be like God in true righteousness and holiness.
— Ephesians 4:22-24 (NIV)

Being "made new" in the attitudes of our minds is not just a natural change, but also a spiritual, supernatural renovation. You are a new creation in Christ! That new wine needs a new wineskin, or paradigm, to live your destiny.

A paradigm is the lens through which we see the world, or our point of view. We think we see the world as it is, but we see the world as we've been conditioned to see it. The right way to change a person's behavior is to change his/her paradigm.[1] *— Stephen Covey*

PARADIGM SHIFTS

Spiritual revelation causes a thought revolution. This results in a shift of paradigm and attitude. This is what the Apostle Paul was teaching in Ephesians 4:25. Our spiritual renewal changes our attitude! No one is more qualified to talk about paradigm shifts than the Apostle Paul. He inherited a worldview that persecuted Christians and mocked their truth, but one day there was a dramatic shift! Revelation knocked him off his donkey on the road to Damascus. Everything shifted with this revelation that Jesus was the Messiah, and He had a better plan for Paul.

Our Father is the master of "aha moments!" Those moments of "seeing the light" cause a revolutionary shift to our paradigm. Revelation displaces our old way of thinking and gives us new lenses to see beyond past limitations. Paul prayed in Ephesians 1:18 that the "eyes of your heart would be enlightened" just as his were. Do you have any donkeys you need knocked off of? I did.

PRAISE SHIFTS PARADIGMS

I grew up in a church that didn't have expressive worship. We held the hymnal and concentrated on following the words. My paradigm was rocked when my family moved across the state and started attending a church that had a "new wine skin" for worship. They raised their hands, danced and sang different choruses with words projected on the wall. Even though I was a young teen, I was stuck in an old paradigm. I loved and respected our new church, but I wasn't going to be forced to join them in their crazy worship!

Then one Sunday night, I got knocked off my donkey and my whole life shifted. I suffered from a painful plantar wart on the bottom of my foot. It was like walking on a stone and getting worse every day. I didn't want to burden my family with the cost of a doctor, so I was trying to cope with it. That night during worship I heard the Lord speak to me, "If you'll dance on it, I'll heal it." I had a choice to make. Did I hold on to my old ideas of worship and stay in my comfort zone, or obey God's voice and dance? I shifted! As I entered into God's presence and began to praise Him, it was like an explosion went off in my soul detonating the limits I had sealed on my heart. I didn't care anymore what people thought. I tasted freedom, and the power of praise cleared out my "stinking thinking" and bad attitude. The next morning my foot was completely healed. Fresh new skin covered where the old nasty sore had been, but the greatest miracle was healing my infected attitude!

Any fact facing us is not as important as our attitude toward it, for that determines our success or failure. The way you think about a fact may defeat you before you ever do anything about it. You are overcome by the fact because you think you are. — Norman Vincent Peale

ATTITUDE IS EVERYTHING

You alone hold the key to your attitude. Paradigms are built on assumptions. When you change those conditioned internal filters that are "futile thinking" and stop assuming limits that aren't true — shift happens! Let your attitude be made new. Let go of old attitudes that are not centered on Christ. Can you hear the Father confidently saying, "Trust me. I've done this a million times; I know what I'm doing. You'll love it, and it will be worth it!"

RETHINK:

⇒ What are the old ways of "futile thinking" you try to cling to?

⇒ Read Ephesians 4:17-31. Write out the fruit of a "darkened mind" and the fruit of a renewed attitude in Christ. Which do you want your legacy to be? Is it worth change?

⇒ What are some conditioned paradigms (formed from parents, culture, education) that place limiting beliefs on you? What revelation do you need to shift these?

RENOVATION PRAYER

Father, today I let go of all my bad attitudes that are centered on my opinions and myself. I pray for revelation that brings a revolution to my thoughts. Knock me off donkeys of limiting thoughts and paradigms that will not take me where you've called. Holy Spirit, show me any paradigms that limit my thinking and affect my attitude. I take control of my emotions and feelings. I hold the key to my attitude, and I yield it to you, Lord. I exalt your truth above my feelings. Make me new

in the attitude of my mind. I am in Christ, and it is in His
name I pray, amen.

DEMOLITION DUMP:
What thoughts need to be dumped out and NOT allowed back?

I'm too scared to change.

AGREEMENT: *What thought focuses your agreement to God's truth today?*

He will help me change. and we can take control.

DAY 7: IT'S YOUR CHOICE

RENOVATION THOUGHT: I CHOOSE THOUGHTS OF LIFE AND CONNECT OTHERS TO
LIFE THROUGH THE FRAGRANCE OF MY LIFE.

*...I have set before you life and death, blessings and curses. Now choose
life, so that you and your children may live. —Deuteronomy 30:19 (NIV)*

L et's celebrate! We've made it through one
week! How's your mind renovation coming?
You are living through demolition and
dreaming about what can be built in the future! Can't
you just see the Father, the master designer and
architect, walking through the rooms and smiling over
the progress?

Be patient. Mind renewal takes time. We've had
wrong thought habits for years, so it's a process of daily
faithfulness to renew those old patterns. I love what Kris
Vallotton says about process. "If you embrace the

promise without the process, you are living in a fantasy."[1]

LIFE BEGINS WITH GOD'S CHOICE

Life begins with God's choice; He chooses you! (Ephesians 1:4)

> *Long before he laid down earth's foundations, he had us in mind, had settled on us as the focus of his love, to be made whole and holy by his love. — Ephesians 1:4 (The Message)*

Then out of His love for us, He gives us our turn to choose. Deuteronomy 30:19 shares how God set the decision before us — choose life or death. Then, He gives us the answer to the test: chose life and you'll be blessed. Our choices begin as options in our brain that we weigh by our values and act out by our decisions. Even present-day habits, the things we now do automatically without thinking, started with a choice.

> I am who I am today because of the choices I made yesterday.
> —Eleanor Roosevelt

LIFE IS DETERMINED BY YOUR RESPONSE

Responsibility is just our *ability* to *respond*. It's your responsibility to change your thoughts. We've heard the classic excuse, "The devil made me do it." The reality is God gave *you* the choice. You can't control the thoughts that tempt, or knock on the door of your mind, but you can choose if you let them stay! The devil tempted Jesus to think evil thoughts, and Jesus chose life. Through His obedience, we too have power to make the right choice!

Dr. Alan Zimmerman writes, "Attitudes have a definite biochemical effect on the body. An attitude of defeat or panic constricts the blood vessels and has a debilitating effect on the entire endocrine system. By contrast, an attitude of confidence and determination activates benevolent therapeutic secretions in the brain."[2]

IF IT'S NOT ON GOD'S MENU, SEND IT BACK!

Imagine going to dinner for a nice meal. The waiter brings you a menu with numerous options and choices. Are you obligated to order everything just because it was on the menu? No! You choose what you order. Are you obligated to eat it just because it's sitting on the plate in front of you? No! You choose what you put in your mouth. The devil will bring lots of dishes to your thought table that you did not order — fear, sickness, anxiety, depression. You have the authority to send them back! When you know it was not on God's menu for your life, send it back!

When thoughts come to your mind, you can learn to accept or reject them. Imagine your thoughts randomly floating across your mind's sky view. You pick which one keeps sailing across and which to let drop down into your mind. No more excuses or blaming others for your thoughts. You alone are responsible for what you choose to think. You can't control your circumstances (or the people around you), but you can control how your circumstances affect you.

YOUR CHOICE SMELLS

Where will you direct your mind—towards life and blessing or death and curses? Our mindset choices determine what fragrance we diffuse around us. The question is not "Do I smell?" but "What do I smell like?" When I put peppermint essential oil in my diffuser at home, the room fills with the fragrance of peppermint. The same is true with our lives, only our mindsets are the diffuser. Whatever thoughts I choose determine the "smell" I emit to those around me. God calls us to be aromatherapy! He wants to "diffuse the fragrance of His knowledge" through us in every place (2 Corinthians 2:14-15, NKJV). Whether we like it or not, our choices affect others. We may live "nose blind" and not realize how our choices smell, but the aroma of our life sticks with other people. Our verse for today says, "Now choose life, so that you and your children may live." Take courage today. Even if you're not motivated to choose life for yourself, choose for your kids, grandkids, nieces and nephews. Choose life, and you will connect others to life!

God created us to think thoughts of life, but he's not going to force us. WE CHOOSE.

TEST (check below):
_____ LIFE
_____ DEATH
(Answer Key: Choose life!)

RETHINK:

⇒ If you could see a "Before / After" picture of your thoughts since Day One how would they compare? What notable changes can you see?

⇒ Is there anything you've been eating that's NOT on God's menu for your life? What can you do to send it back?

⇒ Do the people around you sense an atmosphere of life (positive hope) or death (negativity and dread)?

⇒ What aroma are your mindsets diffusing?

RENOVATION PRAYER

Father, forgive me for making excuses or blaming others for the choices I've made. I take responsibility and will not have a victim mentality. I choose thoughts of life and not death, blessing and not cursing. Let the atmosphere of my life be positive and overflow blessings and encouragement to others. Let my life be the fragrance of Christ. I connect myself to you, the Spirit of life; and I pray today I will connect others to life as well. In Jesus' name, amen.

DEMOLITION DUMP:
What thoughts need to be dumped out and NOT allowed back?

AGREEMENT: *What thought focuses your agreement to God's truth today?*

Phase 2: **FOUNDATIONS**
(FRAME OF MIND)

REBUILDING STRUCTURES AND PATTERNS OF TRUTH

The rain came down, the streams rose, and the winds blew and beat against that house; yet it did not fall, because it had its foundation on the rock. — Matthew 7:25 (NIV)

W elcome to Week Two! With the demo finished, it's time to rebuild a sturdy foundation. Every builder knows the importance of the groundwork to bare the weight of the entire building. Contractors dread hearing the ominous phrase, "It needs foundation repair" because it is expensive and expansive. A crack in the structure provides an unstable infrastructure for everything else built on it.

You don't walk into a house and say, "Wow, this is an impressive foundation!" It only draws attention to itself when it's faulty. It's the same with our spiritual foundations. We don't normally notice them unless there's "structural damage," resulting in sin, shame and sudden ruin. Our spiritual structures are the undergirding principles our life is built on. Our frame of mind frames our life and directs our destiny.

THE OLD COVENANT THOUGHTS

The Genesis garden set the stage for the Father's desire. His heart yearned for a family to walk with, dream with and "do life with." Man and woman, made in His creative image, were like Him. Until, a deceptive thought took root and twisted trust with the inception of a satanic thought. "Did God really say?" (Genesis 3:1) Our spirit connection to the Father was severed with Adam and

They don't notice the little things

Structural damage

foundation sets everything

Eve's choice. The Old Testament establishes our need for a savior to reunite us with God's original intention. The contrast had to be undeniably defined. His sufficiency and our scarcity. His holiness and our depravity. The Old Testament emphasizes the difference between God's thoughts and our thoughts. Isaiah 55:8,9 says, "'For My thoughts are not your thoughts, Nor are your ways My ways,' declares the Lord." He is the potter and we are the clay (Isaiah 64:8). There are no admonitions "to be like God" in the Old Testament, only the stark comparison of our vast difference and our need for a savior.

THE NEW COVENANT DIFFERENCE

Suddenly, everything changes when God became "like us" so we could again "be like Him." The cross ushers in a swift shift back to God's purpose for man — to display His character! [1] Through His death and resurrection, Jesus restored our vital connection to the Father's heart. Now, in Christ, we are challenged to be like Him. That means we can think His thoughts. We have the mind of Christ! The New Covenant redeems God's thoughts back to us.

God became like us,
so that we could be like him again.

Handwritten margin notes: "we always are tempted and looking elsewhere for something else" / "to true and dont change to Please others" / "will your dream get in the way of your walk with God?" / "we have to alter our plans at some point" / "dream life / God"

How about the audacious statement Jesus made that we would even do greater works than He? (John 14:12) This could only be possible with a drastic transformation from our old sinful self to our new creation in Christ. (2 Corinthians 5:17)

Romans 12 provides the blueprint for our foundation repair and mind transformation:

> *Therefore, I urge you, brothers and sisters, in view of God's mercy, to offer your bodies as a living sacrifice, holy and pleasing to God—this is your true and proper worship. **Do not conform to the pattern of this world, but be transformed by the renewing of your mind.** Then you will be able to test and approve what God's will is—his good, pleasing and perfect will.*
> *—Romans 12:1-2 (NIV, emphasis added)*

God doesn't ask us to do something without empowering us to do it. Transformation is possible. We can renew our minds as we walk with Him, dream with Him, converse with Him. The highest level of communication is spirit to Spirit. Now, in Christ, we can have that level of communication reinstated with our Father as Adam and Eve had in the garden. When we receive Jesus as our sin sacrifice that bridges us back to God, we become a living sacrifice filled with His presence. This is not religion trying to live up to a holy God as in the Old Covenant. This is freedom to live in relationship with Him as He comes to live in us. (Remember, He's moving in!)

He is Beging us to not buy into that bad toxic stuff

Dont listen to the worlds standards, listen to **Him**

TAKE UP YOUR TOOL — ATTENTION

During Phase Two of your Mind Renovation, you will take up the tool of ATTENTION while continuing to hold onto your AGREEMENT tool from Phase One. I love the Merriam-Webster's definition of attention, which says, *"the act or state of applying the mind to something."* ATTENTION is a tool of a habitual focus and a set routine. It's like a tape measure, level or plumb line that assures the framework is straight or true. Lack of attention causes slight variations off the intended angles that eventually lead to huge mistakes. Builders ask if the framework is "true," meaning is it level and true to its measurement?

do I listen to the false things too often?

Every day we must give attention to whether our thoughts are level and true.

The Lord asks the shepherd turned prophet, Amos, what he sees in Amos 7:7-8. Amos replies, "The Lord was standing by a wall that had been built true to plumb, with a plumb line in his hand." Israel's attention had waned from God's standard to their own, resulting in their demise. The Lord came with a plumb line in hand to relay the foundation.

The Lord holds a plumb line to rebuild your frame of mind. It is established and aligned with His word His

God says transformation is possible

thoughts toward you. Will you apply your ATTENTION
to see those thoughts come into alignment with His?

*Righteousness and justice are the foundation of your throne; love and
faithfulness go before you. — Psalm 89:14 (NIV)*

I need to hear and take in the
true things about myself, and build
things off eachother. What he has planned
for me to know will shape me. I just
need to know if I will listen and apply
it or just pretend I am when Its not
affecting me. Its what Jesus wants
to give us and it's what he is.
keeps us on the right track. Growing
closer to him and not stray away.
lay foundation build from there,

What pillars do we want when
we are building up.

DAY 8: IS YOUR MIND SET?

RENOVATING THOUGHT: I WILL SET MY MIND ON HEAVEN AND NOT BE PULLED BY DISTRACTING THOUGHTS.

Since, then, you have been raised with Christ, set your hearts on things above, where Christ is, seated at the right hand of God. Set your minds on things above, not on earthly things. For you died, and your life is now hidden with Christ in God. —Colossians 3:1-3 (NIV)

We know how to SET the thermostat to cool the house in the summer heat. We know how to SET the GPS for our road trip destination. We know how to SET the oven temperature to cook the brownies. We watch the Olympic volleyball teams SET the ball for the killer spike.

We can SET a date for the big event. We SET the alarm clock for the next day. Why is it so hard to SET our minds?

DEATH BY DISTRACTION

As a society we are busier with more potential distractions than ever before. We're dinged with notifications, we're buzzed with texts, we're targeted by marketers, we're lobbied for votes and we're hustled by unsolicited emails.

Just as we focus our thoughts to God's calling and commit to follow through with serving our neighbor, loving our spouse and staying positive–SQUIRREL! (You know this inside joke if you've seen the children's movie *Up*. Dug, the yellow dog is wholeheartedly committed to the adventure, until he sees a squirrel. Then all his attention is diverted and his mission abandoned.)

so many distractions What God adventures have you abandoned because of squirrels?

The word "distraction" comes from the French word related to a cruel form of torture reserved for the worst criminals. The offender had his limbs tied to four horses that literally "pulled in all directions" until the person was pulled apart, or "dis-tracted."

This is such a great picture of life today. Distractions pull us in all different ways until we've lost the plot and forgotten our priorities. They divert our ATTENTION (remember that's our tool for foundation repair).

Distractions cause us to put down the level and our balance becomes skewed. As a result, we lose momentum and run in circles from one fleeting thought to another. God's Word encourages us to SET our minds towards heavenly not earthly things.

SET (phronéō in Greek) =
"Set your affection" to direct one's mind to a thing, to seek, to strive for / to be of the same mind i.e. agreed together, cherish the same views, be harmonious / to be of one's party, side with him.[1]

I love this definition for "set." When we set our minds on heavenly things, we place our thoughts in harmony with heaven and cherish the same views. As we pray as Jesus instructed for God's kingdom to come and will be done on earth as in heaven (Matthew 6:9-10), we are praying for heaven's realities to SET our minds in sync with God's eternal perspective, not this earth's temporary feelings. If we have been raised with Christ and seated with Him (in the Spirit), we have a much different perspective! Like flying in a jet above the city rather than being stuck in downtown traffic, our mind is seated in a place of victory and rules over the circumstances and challenges of earth.

Look up, and be alert to what is going on around Christ—that's where the action is. See things from his perspective...your old life is dead. Your new life, which is your real life—even though invisible to spectators—is with Christ in God. He is your life.
— Colossians 3:2-4 (The Message)

SET
YOUR
ATTITUDE
EVERY
MORNING

This is the day the Lord
has made. I will rejoice
and be glad in it.
Ps. 118:24

This is a Marvelous Day!

THIS IS A MARVELOUS DAY!

The best way to SET our mind is by giving our first thoughts every morning to the Lord, whether you're a morning person or not (and I'm not...at all!). When we do this, our minds become SET on God's truth instead of the squirrels vying to steal our attention.

MINDSET = A fixed mental attitude or disposition that predetermines a person's responses to and interpretations of situations. An inclination or a habit. (dictionary.com)

Wouldn't it be amazing if we could SET our MINDS to a predetermined favorable response? Years ago we started a family morning routine to SET our mindset in agreement with God's will. Every morning on the way to school, we would ask our kids to declare with us: "This is a great day! This is a marvelous day! This is the day the Lord has made. I will rejoice and be glad in it!" (Psalm 118:24) Okay, I'll be honest. The kids weren't always enthusiastic as they prayed, but the mind/mouth connection is powerful! Now as adults they continue this beloved family practice.

This became the default address we SET for our mind's destination. It will be a marvelous day because God made it, and we're here breathing it! Likewise, when distractions try to lure you with thoughts of jealousy, anger, insecurity or stress, switch back to the default you SET in the first moments of the day. SET your mind in agreement with heaven's agenda.

A beautiful day begins with a beautiful mindset. When you wake up, take a second to think about what a privilege it is to simply be alive and healthy. The moment you start acting like life is a blessing, I assure you it will start to feel like one. —John Geiger

RETHINK:

⇒ As soon as God gives me a creative word, idea or word for someone else, I write it down or put it in my phone notes. Try doing the same today. As you become a good steward with the thoughts God gives you, He'll multiply them.

⇒ In your journal, write out some circumstances you're dealing with this week, and areas where you are struggling or need a breakthrough. Now, draw an arrow upward. How does God see these things from a heavenly, eternal viewpoint?

⇒ What are the top distractions pulling at your mind's attention? Pray about and write down ways you can guard your mind from them. (Ex. Turn off television, put your phone away, only check emails at certain times, not get involved with gossip, etc.)

⇒ What are some ways you can SET your mind first thing in the morning? (Make a plan and stick to it. It's better to start with something small and be consistent then to have a grandiose plan you can't sustain.)

RENOVATION PRAYER:

Lord, today I set my mind on you. I have died to my old earthly thoughts, and I am alive in Christ and seated with Him. Lord, I pray you would default my mindset to be in harmony and agreement with heaven. Let me see my life through your perspective of victory. Holy Spirit, set a guard on my mind that I will not be pulled by distractions and run in circles. Help me stay focused on the adventures you have destined for me today and not be distracted by the squirrels! This is a great day! This is a marvelous day! This is the day the Lord has made. I will rejoice and be glad in it! In Jesus' name, amen.

ATTENTION: *What thoughts need attention to bring them level with God's truth?*

DAY 9: CONFORMED OR TRANSFORMED?

RENOVATING THOUGHT: I DECIDE IF I WILL BE CONFORMED OR TRANSFORMED BY MY CONSISTENT CHOICES TO LIVE BY THE SPIRIT.

And do not be conformed to this world, but be transformed by the renewing of your mind, that you may prove what is that good and acceptable and perfect will of God. —Romans 12:2 (NKJV)

When I was a kid, I played with a stretchy silicone putty. It could stretch out, conform over shapes and copy the images of any picture it was pressed upon. I saved the colorful Sunday comics, so I could impress my putty on the cartoons.

What images are being impressed onto your mind?

SQUEEZED INTO SHAPE

It's easy and comfortable to conform. Our mind is like silly putty around temporary opinions and media moguls. We buy the clothes the runway says is fashionable; we watch what Hollywood says is entertaining; we laugh at the jokes late night comedians deem uproarious. Every culture and generation has systems and strategies to stereotype and limit. It's like a clown trying to fit into the tiny car of limitations. The devil's agenda involves outside forces of circumstances, media, popular opinion and fear to pressure you into conforming to the shape of this world. His plan is to pressure you from the outside in, but Jesus transforms from the inside out!

When we receive Jesus, our spirit man comes alive in Christ. We stop walking like zombies led by our natural flesh and body. God's ordained flow chart of leadership is spirit to soul (mind, will and emotions) to body. Our spirit (connected to God's Spirit) is the big boss and calls the shots. It releases life into our soul. Our soul is the middleman between our spirit and our body — this is where the work of transformation takes place! Before renewal, your soul called the shots and it's not thrilled to be displaced from power.

Those who live according to the flesh have their minds set on what the flesh desires; but those who live in accordance with the Spirit have their minds set on what the Spirit desires. The mind governed by the flesh is

*death, but the mind governed by the Spirit is life and peace...You,
however, are not in the realm of the flesh but are in the realm of the Spirit,
if indeed the Spirit of God lives in you. — Romans 8:5-9 (NIV)*

TRANSFORMATION TAKES TIME

Our spiritual transformation in Christ is instant when we pray to receive salvation, but our soul transformation, or the renewing of our mind, is a process. Oh, wouldn't it be great if we could snap our fingers, and "Voilà!" Instant growth with no struggle, instant miracle with no faith, instant wisdom with no experience. Wait a minute. What kind of life would that be, with no appreciation for the story that shapes us. Our Father delights in the process, in the small moments and days that shape our character. Even He designed all of creation in an unfolding, beautiful progression. There's an unfolding beautiful progression happening in YOU!

*And I am sure of this, that he who began a good work in you will bring
it to completion at the day of Jesus Christ. — Philippians 1:6 (NIV)*

I love how David Powlison frames it in his article titled, "Sanctification is a Direction":

Grace doesn't follow a schedule...In this life, we can never say: "I've
made it... No more places where I might stumble and fall flat. No more
hard, daily choices to make. No more need for daily grace." Life never
operates on cruise control...The living God seems content to work in
individuals... on a scale of years and decades, throughout a whole
lifetime... There's always something that the Vinedresser is pruning, some

difficult lesson that the Father is teaching the children he loves (John 15; Hebrews 12). It's no accident that "God is love" and "love is patient" fit together seamlessly. God takes his time with us. —David Powlison [1]

JOY IS IN THE JOURNEY

If you've ever watched a home renovation show, you appreciate the transformation more because you saw the starting point and watched the work that went into the process. If you only see the final result with no reference to the struggle — long days, failed inspections, water leaks, and small victories along the way — it all means nothing!

The Greek word for "be ye transformed" is *metamorphoō*, where we get the word "metamorphosis." It would be wonderful if God did all our morphing in a hidden cocoon, like a butterfly, but many times our growing happens out in the open with others watching, like a tadpole (or a house featured on a renovation show). Rather than feel embarrassed by the presence of an audience, be grateful for it! Perhaps it's God's intention to include a crowd in the process, so others can appreciate the product and praise His transforming craftsmanship.

There is joy in the journey of your mind reno! Don't be discouraged with how far you have to go. You've made up your mind, and your thoughts set your direction. All you are responsible for is taking the next step in the right direction.

Forever is composed of nows. —Emily Dickinson

RETHINK:

⇒ What voices conform you to the world? Take inventory of the media outlets vying for your mind space. How do they shape your opinions?

⇒ Can you notice a negative change in your attitude after watching certain things?

⇒ How are you renewing your mind daily to be led by the Spirit?

⇒ Read Romans 8, and write down the keys to your transformation.

⇒ Write down 5 things you've grown in since you started this study.

RENOVATION PRAYER:

Lord, I desire to be led by Your Spirit, and not conformed to the world. Show me where my thoughts have been subject to my culture, generation, race, gender, or nation and not to you! I turn up your voice in my mind. Transform my soul, Lord. Change my mind. Help me to see and celebrate the work in me, and the progress we're making. Today, I pray you would show me a small victory that you are cheering for! In your transforming name I pray, Jesus.

ATTENTION: *What thoughts need attention to bring them level with God's truth?*

DAY 10: REHAB YOUR HABITS?

RENOVATING THOUGHT: GOD WANTS TO REHAB MY HABITS, SO HE CAN COME AND INHABIT THEM.

Above all else, guard your heart, for everything you do flows from it.
—Proverbs 4:23 (NIV)

Let's talk about a word that shapes over 90% of our lives...HABIT. God creatively fashioned our brains to learn something so well it becomes automatic to our subconscious, freeing up more energy. We don't think about how to brush our teeth or tie our shoes–it's automatic.

> HABIT = A recurrent, often unconscious pattern of behavior that is acquired through frequent repetition. (American Heritage Dictionary)

Neuroscience has proven habits form actual ruts in our brain. Our daily habits become a part of the circuitry of our brains. We can make this phenomenon work for our good or for our determent. We form habits, and then our habits form us!

> *We are what we repeatedly do. Excellence, then, is not an act, but a habit.[1]* — *Will Durant*

INGRAINED RESPONSES

I walked into the kitchen as if in a trance, opened the cookie jar and started shoving cookies in my mouth! This was a day of "rehab" for me when the "a-ha!" moment came: my emotional eating was a habit triggered by a subconscious need.

In my book, *Huperwoman[2]*, I share how God healed me nineteen years ago from an unhealthy relationship with food, resulting in a loss of over fifty pounds. Throughout my childhood, I developed many bad habits (formed from wrong thoughts of myself) that led to emotional overeating and eating disorders. My breakthrough came one day when I received a revelation of what was triggering my binges. Habits are like the wheel of a spinning bike; they continue hopelessly spinning until something interrupts the pattern. That day God's voice was like a broom handle thrust into my spinning cycle. My revelation stopped the madness and birthed change.

We were on vacation with our very young children. I was happily watching the kids play outside while my husband golfed with his dad. He called me to say they'd be late returning, which meant I would have to forfeit my shopping time to stay with the kids. Being the good pastor's wife I was, I did not scream and shout my frustrations out on my husband. No, out of habit I walked into the kitchen as if in a trance, opened the cookie jar and started shoving cookies in my mouth! Ironically right before the telephone call I had been reading a book about letting God heal eating disorders. Then the phone rang, and like a response from Pavlov's dogs, I cycled into a habit ingrained in my mind from childhood.

Here is the anatomy of my old destructive habit:
UPSET (trigger) + EAT (routine or habit) = HAPPY (reward)

Charles Duhigg describes the process like this:

This process within our brains is a three-step loop. First, there is a cue, a trigger that tells your brain to go into automatic mode and which habit to use. Then there is the routine, which can be physical or mental or emotional. Finally, there is a reward, which helps your brain figure out if this particular loop is worth remembering for the future.[3]
—Charles Duhigg

These scientific findings reflect scripture well! God rewards those who diligently seek Him. When we receive a revelation of what is the true, real reward and what is only a temporary pleasurable experience, we can begin to rewire our habits.

HABIT LOOP

I believe our failures can sometimes be more of a habit issue than a sin one. These habits need to be renewed and rewired with the Word. Most people don't wake up in the morning thinking, "How can I sin and damage people today?" It's more like the Apostle Paul's words in Romans 7:15, "For what I want to do I do not do, but what I hate I do." (NIV) The Spirit must renew our minds, so the habits of our flesh are rehabilitated.

We all have a variety of habits:

⇒ Social habits (I'm learning to stop interrupting!)
⇒ Financial habits (My husband has me on an Amazon fast. Sigh.)
⇒ Physical habits
⇒ Emotional habits
⇒ Spiritual habits (Prayer and worship are fashioned to become a habit, flowing out of our spirit automatically.)
⇒ Thought habits (These guide all the above!)

Remember-*Sow a thought and reap an action. Sow an action and reap a HABIT. Sow a habit and reap a character. Sow a character and reap a destiny!*

You may be familiar with the idea of rehabilitation from an accident or injury. In physical therapy, people retrain their muscles. The repetition restores them to their useful purpose. One definition of "rehabilitation" is "the conversion of wasteland into land suitable for...habitation." God wants to rehab our habits into ones that He can inhabit!

Think about your habits right now — in your family, in your marriage, in leadership, in your free time. Are there habits of lust, gluttony, gossip, lying or exaggerating? Can God inhabit your habits? Which ones lead you to victory, and which ones lead to chaos and return you to old cycles of regret? It's not too late to retrain your brain with right choices.

RETHINK:

⇒ What unhealthy habits do you need rehab help on?
⇒ Diagram the anatomy of your habit. What is the trigger, the routine and the reward?
⇒ How can you let the Lord heal what triggers your habit?

RENOVATING PRAYER

Dear Lord, I pray that you would rehab my habits. Please reveal to me the ingrained responses and routines I think when I'm triggered by stress or pain. Show me habits of thoughts that lead to actions that aren't transforming my life into your image. I pray you would come and inhabit my habits with the Holy Spirit. In the name of Jesus, amen.

ATTENTION: *What thoughts need attention to bring them level with God's truth?*

DAY 11: REWIRE YOUR BRAIN

RENOVATING THOUGHT: IT IS POSSIBLE TO RETRAIN YOUR BRAIN TO RESPOND WITH HEALTHY HABITS.

Give careful thought to the paths for your feet and be steadfast in all your ways. —Proverbs 4:26 (NIV)

O ur habits are like the electrical wiring behind the walls, which is essential to powering the house. Any unhealthy habit responses must be rewired in order to keep the lights on for the rest of our renovation.

I'm sure you've seen ruts in an old country dirt road. Over time, vehicles take the same path through the ruts, deepening them more and more. The same is true with our thoughts and brains.

Henry David Thoreau described it in his classic, *Walden*:

The surface of the earth is soft and impressible by the feet of men; and so with the paths which the mind travels. How worn and dusty, then, must be the highways of the world, how deep the ruts of tradition and conformity! [1]

When we have a thought it fires neurons that with repetition and consistency form actual ruts in our brains. Scientists agree it's possible to pioneer fresh networks in our brain waves. This principle is paraphrased as, "Neurons that fire together, wire together." [2]

There is good news, naturally and supernaturally! Naturally, God created our brains to rewire themselves. Supernaturally, the Holy Spirit heals those ruts and empowers us to rewire renewed thoughts of truth, in turn rewiring our habits.

We cannot solve our problems with the same thinking we used when we created them. — Albert Einstein

HOW CAN WE REWIRE HABITS?

1. Recognize what needs to change by revelation.

What specific habits would you like to change in your life? Write out the evolution of the habit. What mindset (thought habit) does it stem from? What triggers it? What is the routine that your brain automatically reaches to when triggered? What is the outcome? Now, step further into the future. Where will the path of this habit ultimately lead you? (Unwanted weight? Debt? Divorce?)

2. Refocus on the new routine. (Replace & Repeat!)

"JUST STOP IT" doesn't work! God always calls us to take off (flesh) and put on (righteousness), to come out (of darkness) and bring in (light). We can't just stop a bad behavior; it must be replaced with a positive one. Our brains must rewire to another solution.

> A nail is driven out by another nail; habit is overcome by habit. — Erasmus

Plan out your action or new routine. Write it out — what will you do or say when triggered? Picture it; pray about it.

Yes, I know God can instantaneously deliver people from things and I've seen Him do it! But when people don't replace the old patterns and thoughts with renewed ones, they fall right back into the cycle again. Our brains need new ruts! Those ruts are formed by repetition, by doing the right thing over and over.

3. Revalue how the change will reward you.

It's true; the Bible says that God rewards those who diligently seek Him. Our brains are wired toward their reward.

> But without faith it is impossible to please God; for he that comes to God must believe that he is and that he is a rewarder of those that diligently seek him. — Hebrews 11:6 (KJV)

⇒ What benefits will you receive from the new habit? (Write them down and see them!)

⇒ How will you feel?

⇒ What character does this new habit produce in you?

⇒ How can it open doors for your destiny?

⇒ How will it grow your relationship with the God?

⇒ How will it benefit your family and other significant relationships? Is it something you'd like to pass down as your legacy?

4. Refresh your environment and reinforce with accountability.

Voices determine choices. Be around other people who live out the change you desire. Have you ever noticed when you feel like you're failing your flesh does not want to be around people who are doing what you know you should be doing? Environment feeds desire. Hanging out after midnight online while rewiring a lust addiction is not an environment for success. In my case, doing my daily Bible study at Krispy Kreme wasn't a wise idea. Set yourself up for success not sabotage! Starve the old habit and feed the new routine.

Accountability is the plumb line. It's the alarm clock to protect your attention. It's the assurance that you make the decision that your spirit desires for your eternity, not the temptation that distracts your soul for a few seconds of satisfaction.

Make a decision today that your future self will thank you for!

Every time you make a choice you are turning the central part of you, the part of you that chooses, into something a little different from what it was before. And taking your life as a whole, with all your innumerable choices, all your life long you are slowly turning this central thing into a heavenly creature or into a hellish creature.[3] —C.S. Lewis

RETHINK:

⇒ Look back over the questions under each step of "How to Rewire Your Brain." Write out your answers to each habit you want to rewire.

⇒ Can you see a link or common mindset that feeds different habits? (Ex. Thought: I'm not worthy to succeed. Habit: I sabotage relationships when I start getting close, or I don't take care of myself and eat and exercise right.)

⇒ What are your trigger thoughts? Write out scriptures that speak truth to those thoughts.

RENOVATING PRAYER

Father, You are a creative genius! You created my brain to rewire itself from harmful habits into renewed ones. Holy Spirit, reveal the trigger thoughts to these bad habits and show me how to replace them with truth. Help me change how I see myself. Instead of seeing myself failing, rewrite my story and give me a picture of how you see me overcoming. I pray healing to every harmful rut in my brain. I pray they would never be traveled down again. I pray you would forgive me for every time I've gone down unhealthy, damaging paths. I forgive myself for the wrong choices I've made in the past. I declare today is a new day! In Jesus name, I receive freedom, amen. (Take a minute to sit in His presence and write down some personal words from his heart to yours.)

ATTENTION: *What thoughts need attention to bring them level with God's truth?*

DAY 12: RUNAWAY MIND

RENOVATING THOUGHT: GOD GIVES ME A SOUND MIND AND DELIVERS ME FROM ANXIOUS THOUGHTS.

For God has not given us a spirit of fear, but of power and of love and of a sound mind. —2 Timothy 1:7 (NKJV)

Have you ever heard of the Brooklyn Bridge Elephant Stampede of 1929? Neither had I, but there's a bronze memorial sculpture by Joseph Reginella displayed in New York City's Brooklyn Bridge Park. The official website recalls the tragic day when circus showman P.T. Barnum paraded his elephants across the bridge into Manhattan on the same day as the horrible Wall Street crash. Before they completed their crossing, something spooked the elephants causing a stampede that resulted in the city's most "horrific land mammal tragedy." [1]

WE HAVE A RUNNER!

Fear starts stampedes. Animals can easily "spook" and set off a stampede. Their anxious frenzy sends all the others into total hysteria causing an incident that's thrown out of proportion by panic!

Have you ever had a thought stampede? One small thought spooks you into running swiftly down a track of despair? We also call this the snowball effect. One runaway thought collects others in its breakneck downhill demise.

Your boss simply asks to meet with you and your mind runs to the unemployment line. You hear a faint noise and your mind races to a terrorist invasion. A hangnail becomes open-heart surgery in a matter of 30 seconds. These are all examples of runaway thoughts.

We know it's not logical to be scared or uneasy in our mind, but our emotions don't agree. Has panic ever seized you and caused mass terror? This fear is not a gift from God! The book of James tells us that every good and perfect gift comes from the Father. (James 1:7) Panic is not perfect. Its author is not your Father or friend.

ATTACKED BY PANIC

The National Institute of Mental Health reports that one million Americans will experience panic attack symptoms every month.[2] Have you experienced that "mind monkey" anxiety that ricochets from thought to thought without restraint or logical boundary? Your heart pounds harder, you break out into a sweat, your feel dizzy and sick to your stomach. Finally, you beg God to commandeer the runaway thought train that's heading...faster and faster...for a cliff. Deep breath. Paul mentored his young protégé Timothy by saying, "God has not given us a spirit of fear, but of power and of love and of a sound mind." (2 Timothy 1:7) If God did not give it to us, then we don't want it! Paul said this during one of the most tumultuous times in history when Nero was beheading and burning Christians. Even then, God had not given His children a spirit of panic and phobia, but of love and a sound mind.

Jump off the Thought Train before it derails you!

Has panic ever caused your mind to run away to places it does not belong? Maybe you've heard your spirit whisper, "Don't go there! You know where this line of thinking leads. Jump off this train of thought before it derails you!" It's time to start making your mind obey your spirit, led by the Holy Spirit.

BE STILL AND KNOW

Panic produces runaway mind tracks that lead to destructive behaviors. These tracks need to be boarded up! We have the power in Christ to tell them to stop, to be still and know God. (Psalm 46:10)

When fear comes to bully you and "spook" your thoughts into a stampede, your spirit (guided by the Holy Spirit) can stand up and say, **"No, thoughts, we are not running there!"** Take a step back from these thoughts and realize they are not a part of you! They do not have permission to seep into your soul!

PANIC CAUSES OUR THOUGHTS TO STAMPEDE. *Love settles them to be still.*

Fear thoughts are displaced only when replaced with love thoughts. You can tell yourself all day "Don't be afraid," but until you replace the fear with love, there's no track for your mind to run on.

There is no fear in love. But perfect love drives out fear, because fear has to do with punishment. The one who fears is not made perfect in love.
— *1 John 4:18 (NIV)*

Can you recognize any dark thought tunnels that need to be boarded up? The Holy Spirit has given you power to overcome panic. By trusting in God's love, you can calm those fear thoughts with a disciplined mind that's able to be still–and not make a run for it!

STAMPEDE FABRICATION

Oh wait, I almost forgot ... there was no Brooklyn Bridge Elephant Stampede; it's all an elaborate fabrication. Yes, there is an official-looking website, walking tour, $30 t-shirts and a beautiful bronze memorial to an imaginary incident. But, Reginella's imagination "ran away" with him. His convoluted scheme tricks tourists into wasting time on a fantasy when they should be discovering the real treats in the Big Apple.

Can you see how the devil has tried to fabricate panic to send your life into pandemonium? It's not true. Be still. See God's truth. Your life is too precious and your true destiny too great to be sidelined by fictitious fears and runaway "what if" fantasies.

RETHINK:

⇒ What triggers your runaway thoughts into stampedes?
⇒ How does fear or panic threaten your mind? What is the lie? What is God's truth?

⟹ How can you board up those thought tracks so that you never run down them again?

⟹ Do you say things like, "I'm losing my mind!" or "I'm crazy!" Displace those negative confessions with true statements like, "Peace guards my mind. I have a sound mind through Christ's power."

⟹ Many times when our mind tries to run away, it's beneficial to get up and do something to shift our fixation, such as take a walk, play an instrument, or read a good book. What healthy habits could help calm your monkey mind?

RENOVATING PRAYER

Father, I believe you are the author of good and perfect gifts. Fear is not from you I no longer receive it. I won't continue to live with runaway thoughts. I take authority in Jesus' name over every spirit of fear and anxiety making me think I'm crazy and losing my mind. Right now, Jesus, board up every non-productive, dead end, destructive track in my mind and empower me to never cross over them again! I declare I have a sound, disciplined and calm mind. I will be still and know that you are God. Be exalted in every thought and every action of my life. In Jesus name, I pray, amen.

ATTENTION: *What thoughts need attention to bring them level with God's truth?*

DAY 13: HEALING MEMORIES

RENOVATING THOUGHT: THE REDEEMING POWER OF JESUS HEALS OUR NEGATIVE MEMORIES.

For I know the thoughts that I think toward you, says the Lord, thoughts of peace and not of evil, to give you a future and a hope.
—Jeremiah 29:11 (KJV)

A utumn is my favorite time of the year, with its falling leaves, football games, cooler weather and, of course, pumpkin spice lattes! I recently heard a story about a lady who hates pumpkin spice lattes. When she was a little girl her dad made pumpkin spice bread for the family. Instead of adding baking powder, he used baking soda! The bread smelled heavenly, but it tasted salty and rancid. Today whenever she thinks of trying anything with pumpkin spice, her mind runs to that first bad experience. Her brain classifies and judges all pumpkin spice items as distasteful. She needs memory redemption. I wish I could invite her to the coffee shop!

How many of us do the same thing? If we've experienced a painful incident, we judge everything associated with that event as painful and label it as dangerous. This is the precursor of prejudice — judging all by the actions of a few. *I got hurt in church, thus all churches are hurtful. A man abused me; all men are abusive. My boss was unfair; all bosses are out to get me.* You get the idea.

FILTERS THAT FOG THE FUTURE

You've just discovered the devil's major scheme to steal our futures. He tries to trick us into judging one negative incident as life's foregone conclusion. Every time we encounter something that reminds us of the initial incident, we automatically place a filter over it that prevents a truthful view. The power of that pain perpetuates a continued cycle.

We don't see things as they are, we see them as we are. —Talmud

I have a close friend who was stalked and harassed at work by a Romanian man. Any time she heard of someone being from Romania, an instant invisible filter from her past hurt superimposed onto the new person. In the early 1990s communism fell in Romania, and we were blessed to participate in many ministry trips to evangelize during this vibrant time. My friend had a choice that would greatly impact her destiny and the good plans God had for her. Would she let God heal her filter of Romanian people and redeem her painful past or stay stuck in that memory? It was her choice. Thankfully, she chose healing and saw God birth a beautiful love for the Romanian people in her heart! That divine appointment would have been thwarted if she had not made the choice to forgive and redeem the hurt.

WHO ARE YOU ENTERTAINING IN YOUR HEAD?

Memories are powerful and real. Smells, sounds or a feeling can trigger them. How many painful memories occupy real estate in your head? Maybe someone lied to you twenty years ago. You never see them anymore, but because you hold onto the negative memory, it's like they are still a part of your life, sitting down in your mind for coffee and tense conversations.

As the years go by, our minds get packed with all the people who've hurt us. Every time we rehearse the memory of the hurt, we reinforce the strength of its hold on us, turning the memory into a "stronghold." God did not create you to be tormented by your memories. Your past does not define your future.

But God will redeem my soul from the power of the grave: for he shall receive me. Selah. — Psalm 49:15 (KJV)

LET IT LOOSE

The Hebrew word for "redeem" means, "to loose by cutting or severing, to pay a price for, to let go, to set free." [1]

We can't change what's happened to us, but we can let the Lord redeem those memories and strip their power to haunt us. As we make the decision to let it go and forgive, Jesus severs the tie to the painful memory. Forgiveness isn't a feeling, but a choice to be free. Dr. Caroline Leaf shares how bitterness actually chains us to that person and event in our mind:

Forgiveness is a choice … it enables you to release all those toxic thoughts of anger, resentment, bitterness, shame, grief, regret, guilt and hate. These emotions hold your mind in a nasty, vice-like grip. Most importantly, as long as these unhealthy toxic thoughts dominate your mind, you will not be able to grow new healthy thoughts and memories.[2]

We may feel that by forgiving someone, we validate his or her behavior. But, forgiveness doesn't excuse others' behavior; it keeps their behavior from destroying our heart. **It frees us from their actions and leaves their sin in the hands of God, not in our heads!**

It is often quoted, "Un-forgiveness is like drinking poison and expecting the other person to die." Are you ready to stop the toxic past from ruling your future? The blood of Jesus not only blots out our sins but the sins of others.

Make allowance for each other's faults, and forgive anyone who offends you. Remember, the Lord forgave you, so you must forgive others.
Colossians 3:13 (NLT)

REDEEM THE MEMORY

A few years ago my husband and I went to a special restaurant for a date night. We were tired, and the evening turned into a big argument. We worked it out, but every time I drove by that restaurant the memories of that disgruntled night filled my mind. Finally, I told my husband we needed to redeem that restaurant in my memory! We had a wonderful evening and replaced the negative memory with a positive one. Now I can drive by and smile at how I overcame.

It may take time to remove the filters, but if you know God is with you in that memory, then you can trust Him to lead you out of it. Jesus redeems our memories so they don't replay in our minds like broken records. We can't change the facts of what happened to us, but we can change our response and embrace the truth of God's healing. The framework for your thought life is built on forgiveness: Christ loving you, and Christ loving through you. For every painful memory distorting the flavor of your life (like the bad pumpkin spice bread!), there is redeeming power to set us free to taste a pleasant future.

RETHINK:

⇒ Do haunting memories play over and over in your thoughts?

⇒ Who do you "entertain" in your mind that needs to be shown the front door?

⇒ Is there anyone you need to forgive in order to let it go? Stop right now and make a decision to forgive.

⇒ Are there things you have judged because you had a negative first experience? Invite Jesus into that memory and let Him speak truth to the lies that are filtering your future.

RENOVATING PRAYER

Lord, I believe your redeeming power can cut me loose from the past and sever every evil, painful memory from my mind. I pray for the blood of Jesus to cover those memories. I no longer see it the same; I see it red - covered in your blood. You paid the price for my freedom. You forgave me so that I can forgive others. Lord, help me to forgive _____ for how they hurt me. I release them and let go of the recordings I have replayed over and over in my mind. Thank you for setting me free! I make a choice to remove this filter from my future. I pray you would redeem and exchange my negative memories with new positive ones. I receive beauty for the ashes of my past. (Isaiah 61:3) In Jesus' name, amen.

ATTENTION: *What thoughts need attention to bring them level with God's truth?*

DAY 14: DOUBLE MIND DECLINE

RENOVATING THOUGHT: I WILL SERVE THE LORD WITH SINGLE HEART AND MIND.

A double minded man is unstable in all his ways... Therefore submit to God. Resist the devil and he will flee from you. Draw near to God and He will draw near to you. Cleanse your hands, you sinners; and purify your hearts, you double-minded. —James 1:8 (KJV); 4:7-8 (NKJV)

Read this excerpt from my book, *Huperwoman*:

"Picture Peter accepting Jesus' invitation to step out of the boat and walk to him...Faith arose in Peter as he heard Jesus' word to him, for faith comes by hearing. He stepped out, defied the impossible and operated in an anointing beyond what he had ever experienced before—until the wind began to blow.

When the storm surged, his focus shifted from Jesus to the squall. He wavered as the waves rose..." [1]

THOUGHT BUBBLES

We know this story in Matthew 14 well. If we could see the thought bubbles above Peter's head, perhaps they'd look something like this ...

"Jesus? Is that you? You want me to walk out there to you? Wow! This will be fun! I'm doing it. I'm coming Jesus! Whoa...I'm walking on water. I hope everyone's seeing this! This is so cool! Wow, those waves are really high. I didn't realize the wind was blowing so hard. What was I thinking? Men can't walk on water. How do I get myself into these things? I'm going to drown. Jesus, save me!"

Peter went from confident wonder to colossal waver in a matter of seconds. Have you been there? Maybe you stepped out of your comfort zone full of faith. Your thoughts are positive, reassuring your decision. Then you hit a bump in the road. This is not what you expected. Life's unfolding circumstance does not match up with your proposed scenario. Then you start second thinking your decision. Fearful thoughts of failure creep in and doubt tempts your faith. The devil provides a multitude of reasons why you'll fail and shouldn't trust God.

SECOND THINKING DOUBT

Peter saw the boisterous wind and was afraid, but later Jesus did not ask him why he was afraid—He asked him why he DOUBTED!

> We can doubt without having to live a doubting way of life. Doubt encourages rethinking. Its purpose is more to sharpen the mind than to change it. Doubt can be used to pose the question, get an answer and push for a decision. But doubt was never meant to be a permanent condition. Doubt is one foot lifted, poised to step forward or backward. There is no motion until the foot comes down
> (Life Application Study Bible). [2]

Many people needlessly suffer condemnation when they have a thought of temptation or doubt. Even Jesus was tempted. Thoughts come and go. **You will have thoughts of doubt; the question is will they have you?** Doubts are not meant to be the end of the story, but rather the end of our own strength. When we come to the end of ourselves and submit to God, then when the storms blow hard and things don't look like we imagined, we still stand strong!

> As my mind can conceive of more good, the barriers and blocks dissolve. My life becomes full of little miracles popping up out of the blue.
> — Louise L. Hay

UNDIVIDED ATTENTION

The problem comes when we compartmentalize and divide our heart, which results in confusion and instability. David prayed for the Lord to give him an undivided heart, which in Hebrew is the word *leb*. It means, "inner self, will, mind."

> Teach me your way, LORD, that I may rely on your faithfulness; give me an undivided heart, that I may fear your name. — Psalm 86:11 (NIV)

The Bible warns against spiritual schizophrenia, or double mindedness. Our thoughts try to divide into two sides: doubt and faith. Our minds cannot stay balanced between doubt and faith; the loudest one will sway the other. Sadly, this is average Christian behavior in many churches. One Sunday they are "all in" and excited about serving God, and the next they're a completely different person. Double vision causes confusion and chaos. A path must be chosen, a direction charted.

FOUNDATION OF FAITH

It's interesting how the Holy Spirit inspired James to bring back the metaphor of waves as a picture of doubt and double mindedness. The King James Version says that he who wavers between faith and doubt is like a wave "driven" and "tossed" with the wind.

If you don't know what you're doing, pray to the Father. He loves to help. You'll get his help, and won't be condescended to when you ask for it. Ask boldly, believingly, without a second thought. People who "worry their prayers" are like wind-whipped waves. Don't think you're going to get anything from the Master that way, adrift at sea, keeping all your options open. — James 1:4-8 (The Message)

We are building a foundation of faith into our renovated life. That faith demands a decision. It doesn't "keep all the options open" and deliberate between man's opinions and God's. It's a clear choice. Jesus gave renovation tips on how to build a strong foundation in the book of Matthew:

Therefore whoever hears these sayings of Mine, and does them, I will liken him to a wise man who built his house on the rock: and the rain descended, the floods came, and the winds blew and beat on that house; and it did not fall, for it was founded on the rock.
— Matthew 7:24-25 (NKJV)

Faith comes from hearing the Word of God. (Romans 10:17) As we feed our faith with God's Word, our obedience (and subsequently a strong foundation) will result. Stand strong.

RETHINK:

⇒ Have you noticed that your thoughts divide into two sides: doubt and faith?
⇒ Which are you feeding, and which are you starving?

⇒ What are you doing to feed your faith? What are some things you can do today?

⇒ Do you give more weight to man's/culture's opinions or God's?

RENOVATING PRAYER

Lord, I submit and humble my thoughts before you. I rely on your faithfulness where my faith is weak and doubts. Give me an undivided heart and mind. Help me, Father, to sift out thoughts of doubt. Rebuild a strong foundation of faith in my mind. I pray that when storms blow and my faith foundation is shaken, it will not be moved! Empower me to serve you with a single heart and mind. Let faith always be my frame of mind. In Your faithful name I pray, amen.

ATTENTION: *What thoughts need attention to bring them level with God's truth?*

Phase 3: INTERIOR FURNISHINGS

(DÉCOR AND MORE)

RELEASING CREATIVITY AS YOU ARRAY YOUR INNER THOUGHTS WITH GOD'S ABUNDANCE.

And we have received God's Spirit (not the world's spirit), so we can know the wonderful things God has freely given us. 1 Corinthians 2:12 NLT

Welcome to **Week Three!** Now we are getting to the fun part! So much time and effort goes into demolition and frameworks, but now we get to focus on the fun things that you see and enjoy, like paint colors, style and all the interior furnishings. These are the things that make a house a home. Or, the things that make you, YOU!

We are enlisting the skills of the most proficient designer in the universe! Think about our Father's creative spectrum. His portfolio displays a vast gamut, from oceans to orcas, constellations to cellular structures, Mount Everest to YOU!

FOR WE ARE GOD'S MASTERPIECE. HE HAS CREATED US ANEW IN CHRIST JESUS, SO WE CAN DO THE GOOD THINGS HE PLANNED FOR US LONG AGO.

Ephesians 2:10
NLT

Jesus advertised His mission to give us life and life more abundantly! (John 10:10) **That abundant life starts**

108

in your beautiful mind. Yes, you are called to have a beautiful mind and heart — your internal dwelling, a sanctuary reflecting God's glory, filled with the Holy Spirit and exhibited to the world in love.

A beautiful mind creates a beautiful life.

TAKE UP YOUR TOOL: ARTISTRY

We've used the tools of AGREEMENT and ATTENTION. Now it's time for our third tool: ARTISTRY! **This tool is like a paintbrush that adds color and style to the ideas that flow from your mind.** It manifests in words of life, creative ideas, positivity and generosity. It decorates our life in glorious, living color that foreshadows our future home in heaven. This artistry is fueled by our relationship with the Holy Spirit. He is here as our collaborator, our spark of inspiration.

No eye has seen, no ear has heard, and no mind has imagined what God has prepared for those who love Him. But it was to us that God revealed these things by His Spirit. For His Spirit searches out everything and shows us God's deep secrets. No one can know a person's thoughts except that person's own spirit, and no one can know God's thoughts except God's own Spirit. And we have received God's Spirit (not the world's spirit), so we can know the wonderful things God has freely given us.
— 2 Corinthians 2:10 - 12 (NLT)

Over the next seven days, we will furnish our minds with things God has prepared for us, things the Holy Spirit reveals. The Holy Spirit searches the heart of the Father and reveals those secret thoughts to us as we open our minds to Him. Let's go shopping in the spirit! You have a gift card ready to redeem.

DAY 15: SCARCITY THINKING

RENOVATING THOUGHT: GOD WANTS TO TRANSFORM MY MENTALITY FROM SCARCITY TO ABUNDANCE.

Beloved, I pray that you may prosper in all things and be in health, just as your soul prospers. —3 John 2 (NKJV)

I magine a thirsty, dry plant in need of a major summer soaking. Suddenly, the rain begins to fall, drip after glorious drip of life-giving refreshment. The downpour bestows provision to the plant, but it is not received. Why? Because of the umbrella shielding the hardened earth from the downpour.

What umbrella do you hold that hinders the downpour of God's thoughts and provision for you?

DO YOU HOLD UMBRELLAS OF LIMITATION?

The Holy Spirit searches the mind of God and desires to pour out these revelations to us. (2 Corinthians 2:9-10) But our limiting mindsets shield us from these revelations like an umbrella blocking the downpour of His Spirit. Our umbrellas become excuses that prevent us from experiencing abundant life.

Umbrellas often start with words like, "I'm too ..." or "I'm not enough." Do any of these umbrellas sound familiar: *I couldn't do that because I owe too much money. I can't dream that because I'm too old. I couldn't try that because I'm too scared.*

God pours His thoughts and dreams out, and we put our hands over the cup saying, "Oh, no thank you. I couldn't possibly have that." Our cup is empty and in great need of refilling, but we stop the downpour and keep God's ideas at bay because we're afraid of the unknown, afraid His ideas are too good to be true.

What we have received is not the spirit of the world, but the Spirit who is from God, so that we may understand what God has freely given us.
— 2 Corinthians 2:12 (NIV)

The real question is: What does God think? What is He trying to download by His Spirit to you? What have you been missing out on because you've walled off His Spirit with your limiting beliefs?

THE GLASS IS REFILLABLE

Steping out
better relationship

The theme of a scarcity thinker is, "There's never enough!" Many people argue whether the glass is half empty or half full, but a child of God knows the glass is refillable! He is a faithful God, and He doesn't have His provision power on ration!

People who wonder if the glass is half full or empty have missed the point. It's refillable!

Scarcity thinking is the new buzzword for what we formerly called a "poverty mentality." This line of thinking focuses on what you don't have instead of being

thankful for what you do have. It's an underlying panic
that you will run out and better "get all you can and can
all you get!"

> Are your thoughts focused on what you have
> or on what you're missing?

FILTER OF FEAR

Scarcity thinking affects much more than finances. It's a
filter of fear that zaps the vibrancy out of today's
blessing. It says: *I can't forgive; I don't have enough
grace. I can't celebrate your win because it takes away
from mine.*

Someone else's blessing does not negate God's
provision for you. Can you see what the lie of scarcity
produces? A small-minded, stingy, fearful person. This
is not your inheritance as a child of God! There is room
at the table for you.

Brené Brown says in her book, *Daring Greatly*, "We
live in a culture of 'perceived scarcity' that says, there's
never enough. We start off the morning thinking we
didn't get enough sleep, go through the day thinking we
don't have enough time and fall asleep thinking we failed
to accomplish enough tasks. Whatever we have, do, or
get, it's never enough." [1]

Michael Hyatt gives these descriptions of abundance
versus scarcity thinkers on his blog:

SCARCITY THINKERS:
- ⟹ Believe there will never be enough.
- ⟹ Are stingy with their knowledge, contacts and compassion.
- ⟹ Default to suspicion and find it difficult to build rapport.
- ⟹ Resent competition, believing it makes the pie smaller and them weaker.
- ⟹ Ask themselves, How can I get by with less than is expected?
- ⟹ Are pessimistic about the future, believing that tough times are ahead.
- ⟹ Think small, avoiding risk.
- ⟹ Are entitled and fearful.

ABUNDANCE THINKERS:
- ⟹ Believe there is always more where that came from.
- ⟹ Share their knowledge, contacts and compassion with others.
- ⟹ Default to trust and build rapport easily.
- ⟹ Welcome competition, believing it makes the pie bigger and them better.
- ⟹ Ask themselves, How can I give more than is expected?
- ⟹ Are optimistic about the future, believing the best is yet to come.
- ⟹ Think big, embracing risk.
- ⟹ Are thankful and confident. [2]

MIND BLOWN!

God's plan is to bless us, so that He can bless others through us! Abundance thinking affects every area of your life from friends, to food, to the future. There is more than enough! If it's not in our checking account today, rejoice because this is not your final destination!

Read the Apostle Paul's words to the Philippians:

> *... I have learned to be content whatever the circumstances. I know what it is to be in need, and I know what it is to have plenty. I have learned the secret of being content in any and every situation, whether well fed or hungry, whether living in plenty or in want. I can do all this through him who gives me strength. — Philippians 4:11-13 (NIV)*

Paul's thinking didn't change with his circumstance. The wealth of Paul's spirit overflowed with joy and gratitude into this soul. His spirit was synced into the truth of his rich, eternal abundance in Christ and that gave him great strength!

If you knew what abundant, refillable resources the Father has for you, you'd jump up and down like a little kid! Jesus told us to pray, "Your Kingdom come, your will be done, on earth as it is in heaven." (Matthew 6:10 NIV) Heaven abounds with provision; earth should secure that supply! Let the giver of the best gifts blow your mind with His extravagant love.

> *Consider the kind of extravagant love the Father has lavished on us— He calls us children of God! — 1 John 3:1*

What would you love to furnish your internal house with but were afraid to ask for? Remove any limiting umbrellas that hinder His outpouring of abundance and let's starve all scarcity thinking!

RETHINK:

⇒ What areas do your thoughts tend toward scarcity instead of abundance? (Ex. time, money, friends, talents)

⇒ Read the Parable of the Talents. Who had a scarcity mentality? (Matthew 25:14–30)

⇒ What "perceived scarcity" are you making your reality when God has a bigger plan?

⇒ Pray about how you can bless someone else today. The best way to starve scarcity thinking is by giving to others.

RENOVATING PRAYER

Lord, send a deluge of your Spirit to reveal your thoughts towards me. Enlarge my capacity to see the unseen things you've prepared uniquely for me. I repent for any mindset that limits your rule and reign in my mind. Help me think your abundant thoughts. Father, thank you for your good and perfect gifts. I ask you to pour out your blessing on my family, and me that we may bless others. You care for me and have made a plan for provision. I declare there's more than enough _____ (fill in your blank). In the name of Jesus, amen.

 ARTISTRY: *What beautiful thought is the Holy Spirit inspiring in the décor of your mind?*

DAY 16: NEUTRALIZE THE NEGATIVE

RENOVATING THOUGHT: POSITIVE THOUGHTS MAKE US HEALTHIER—SPIRIT, SOUL AND BODY.

But we do not belong to those who shrink back and are destroyed, but to those who have faith and are saved. —Hebrews 10:39 (NIV)

In life two negatives don't make a positive. So why does it seem easier to critique than to compliment? Why do we remember negative comments more than positive ones? Why are we drawn more to defaming gossip than good news? Why are there sixty-two percent more emotionally negative words in the English dictionary than there are positive ones?

Scientists say it is our natural negativity bias.

NEGATIVITY BIAS

Because of negativity bias, "Things of a more negative nature (e.g. unpleasant thoughts, emotions, or social interactions; harmful/traumatic events) have a greater effect on one's psychological state and processes than do neutral or positive things." [1]

For efficiency's sake, our brains only store negative and positive experiences, not neutral ones. All the neutral things are forgotten and not filed as important. When the brain encounters bad news, it immediately stores it in long-term memory. In contrast, positive experiences must be held in our awareness for over 12 seconds in order for the transfer from short-term to long-term memory to take place. Rick Hanson describes it this way: *"The brain is like Velcro for negative experiences, but Teflon for positive ones."* [2]

You may have experienced this yourself. For example, you spend a lovely day with a friend or your spouse. You visit your favorite coffee shop and belly laugh over funny moments from the week. You attend a lovely matinee movie followed by dinner and dessert at your favorite restaurant. While driving home, you argue over a misunderstanding and end the day feeling deflated. Though you had many more positive experiences that day than negative, the negative stands out stronger to your emotions. This is the negativity bias.

Negative thoughts stick around because we believe them, not because we want them or choose them. —Andrew Bernstein

I'm not sure if this bias is a result of the fall of man, or, as many scientists suggest, a survival mechanism to protect man from impending danger. Either way, we have a natural propensity toward the negative, which needs the power of God's truth to counteract it.

THE 5:1 RATIO

Most experts agree that we need five positive interactions to counteract every one negative. Dr. Gottman and Robert Levenson studied married couples in the 1970s and predicted which couples would divorce based on a ratio of positive to negative interactions. After following up nine years later, they were ninety percent accurate. They discovered that as long as there were five times as many positive interactions between partners as negative, the relationship remained stable.[3]

Are you counting your conversations today? How many positive interactions have you had to counteract the negative?

Tell the negative committee that meets inside your head to sit down and shut up. — Ann Bradford

YOUR THOUGHTS CAN KILL YOU

Scientists stagger at the mind's ability to produce its internal projections. You can actually "think yourself" sick. In a trial for Parkinson's disease, participants were informed about the possible side effects with their medical trial. Even though they were only given a placebo, sixty-five percent reported adverse conditions as a result. This is known as a "nocebo"–a negative placebo effect.[4] The word "nocebo" comes from the Latin *noceo*, which means, "I shall harm."

The devil always tries to make his nocebo ("I shall harm") effects appear stronger than God's truth in our lives! With brains that are naturally drawn to negatives, it's important to focus our thoughts on truth.

A.N.T.

Address Negative
Thoughts

LET'S RETHINK OUR APPROACH TO NEUTRALIZING THE NEGATIVE:

⇒ Interject your day with gratitude. Keep a journal of things you're grateful for. Stop to say "thank you" at the top of every hour of the day. When any negative thought or worry comes to mind immediately thank God for His promises.

⇒ Insert small, pleasant experiences throughout your day, instead of only waiting for the weekend, vacations or birthdays. Experts agree that multiple small positive experiences throughout the day combat the negative more significantly than one big one.

⇒ Celebrate small benchmarks throughout a project rather than waiting until its completion.

⇒ Praise five times more than you complain! All throughout the book of Psalms, we see negative counteracted with praise: "As for me, I will always have hope; I will praise you more and more." Psalm 71:14 (NIV) As we sing and praise for longer than twelve seconds, it sends the positive from short-term to long-term memory.

In Christ's redemptive power, we are not limited to the negativity bias. The Gospel is the Good News that overcomes all past, present and future bad news! As the

Holy Spirit (not our carnal minds) leads, we will see and speak positive truth that neutralizes the enemy.

> Negativity —it can only affect you if you're on the same frequency. Vibrate higher. —Author Unknown

RETHINK:

⇒ Is your personality naturally positive, or do you tend to be cynical?

⇒ Was the atmosphere of your home growing up positive or negative? How does this filter your thoughts?

⇒ How is the ratio (five positive to one negative) in your significant relationships?

⇒ How can you help create a positive work environment at your job?

⇒ How can this information impact you as a parent? A spouse? An employee?

RENOVATING PRAYER:

Father, forgive me for my negative thoughts and words. Thank you for the life of Jesus and for His Spirit who gives me life and the ability to think and speak positively. I declare I will not live by my natural flesh and negative appetites. I belong to You, Lord. Help me to lean not on my own understanding; give me your thoughts. In the name of Your Son, Jesus, amen.

ARTISTRY: *What beautiful thought is the Holy Spirit inspiring in the décor of your mind?*

DAY 17: SELF-TALK SABOTAGE

RENOVATING THOUGHT: I AM GOD'S WORK OF ART, AND MY SELF-TALK WILL HONOR HIS CRAFTSMANSHIP.

I will praise You, for I am fearfully and wonderfully made. Marvelous are Your works and that my soul knows very well. —Psalm 139:14

You stupid idiot! You never do anything right! You're the ugliest person ever! You're such a failure! You're a sorry excuse for a human being! I hate you! You always mess everything up!

Most people (let's hope) would never shout these venomous words to someone else but easily disparage themselves in their own self-talk.

Thinking: the talking of the soul with itself. — Plato

INTERNAL SOUND SYSTEM

God is rewiring your sound system in your remodeled mind to play lovely conversations and background music. It's amazing how sound creates an atmosphere. When our house was for sale, I played soothing, anointed music during showings. The buyer who purchased our house said, "When I walked into your house, it hugged me." I had created an environment that connected with her emotions. We do this with our internal sound every day.

WHEN YOU INSULT YOURSELF IT'S REALLY A CRITICISM OF THE *Creator*

PSALM 139

Whether you realize it or not, you talk to yourself. Your internal house is wired for sound, and that sound sets the environment for your mood. It originates in your thoughts, resonates throughout your body and overflows out of your mouth. This internal monologue is referred to as your "self-talk." Here you provide the running commentary and evaluation of how you're doing in life. Your inner chatter is shaping your life and eventually even affecting how other people see and treat you.

Self-degradation is not a form of modesty; it will only serve to weaken your spirit. — Author Unknown

CRITIQUING GOD'S ART

Can you imagine someone approaching the priceless Mona Lisa with a big black marker and scribbling obscenities over her? What if someone vandalized Michelangelo's renowned David sculpture? It's certain handcuffs would follow those actions. Yet, we degrade God's work of art without conscience.

For we are God's handiwork, created in Christ Jesus to do good works, which God prepared in advance for us to do. — Ephesians 2:10 (NIV)

Every work of art represents its creator. No human has the qualifications to critique God's work. When you insult yourself, it's really a criticism of your Maker. The same artist who created the Grand Canyon, Mount Everest and Victoria Falls designed you. Let's give Him some credit by not discrediting ourselves! If you're a parent, you may know the agony of hearing your own child degrade himself. Can you imagine how it hurts God's heart to hear you speak negatively about yourself—the apple of His eye? (Psalm 17:8)

CONVERSATION CONVERSION

The Bible speaks clearly about encouraging conversations. We usually only see these instructions for our words towards others, but could they be intended for our self-talk as well?

Don't use foul or abusive language. Let everything you say be good and helpful, so that your words will be an encouragement to those who hear them. — Ephesians 4:29 (NLT)

Let your conversation be always full of grace, seasoned with salt, so that you may know how to answer everyone. — Colossians 4:6 (NIV)

It's interesting that Paul suggests in Colossians that our conversation be full of grace (God's favor towards us) and seasoned with salt. In antiquity and in developing nations today, salt is highly prized. It has many uses besides just giving food flavor. It prevents decay by acting as a preservative, it removes stains and rust, it aids in healing and it eliminates odors. Does your seasoned self-talk do these things: give flavor and fun to the mundane, preserve and save you from decaying doubt, remove stains of failure, help heal your heart and eliminate the "stinking thinking" odor? If not, it's time to update and convert your sound system!

To update and convert, we must know God's thoughts for us. This is a daily process that begins with discovering yourself in His Word. In Luke 4, Jesus walks into the temple, reads Isaiah 61:1-2, proclaims this scripture is now fulfilled and sits down. (Drop the mic.) Jesus found himself in The Word. Of course he was the living expression of the Word, but on that day in front of the negative cynics, He pointed to His purpose in Scripture and "found himself" there. Have you found yourself in God's Word? The Holy Spirit reveals where you are in God's heart. He reveals that God's promises are for you and about you!

Find yourself in the Word, and you'll find your future.

STANDARD FEATURES AND CUSTOM UPGRADES

My husband and I built a house a few years ago. It was important to know which items came *standard* from that builder and which were costly custom upgrades. My dad is a contractor and owns a construction company. He often sways customers from the competition because he generously offers standard features like granite countertops, stainless steel appliances and Jacuzzi tubs. The Father, your renovation contractor, has generously given all His children amazing *standard features*— general promises for all of His children, like inheritance as His heir, eternal salvation, peace of mind, righteousness friendship with God. (Read the "I Am Promises" in the appendix.)

These standard features blow your mind with God's goodness, but there's more. To each unique creation, He also gives custom built-ins and upgrades! These are uniquely instilled in you for your specific calling and destiny. Have you ever seen people tour a home and remark, "Wow, I love the charm and the character!" Those are upgrades; and yes, you have them.

In his grace, God has given us different gifts for doing certain things well. — Romans 12:6 (NLT)

You discover these "built-ins" by learning more about your spiritual gifts (1 Corinthians 12, Ephesians 4, Romans 12), personality, strengths, talents and individual calling. The Holy Spirit is waiting to reveal them to you; it's your job to learn, appreciate and use them for His Kingdom. (Matthew 25:14-30)

THINKING TOO HIGHLY

Some people fear thinking good thoughts towards themselves results in pride. It's even taught in some religious circles that degrading self-talk is holy. Pride is a preoccupation with self, positive or negative. As Rick Warren says, "True humility is not thinking less of ourselves, but thinking of ourselves less." [1]

Love the Lord your God with all your heart and with all your soul and with all your mind and with all your strength. The second is this: Love your neighbor as yourself. There is no commandment greater than these. —
Matthew 12:30-31 (NIV)

As we give our mind to loving God, instead of hating or exalting ourselves, freedom comes to love others. A healthy love for ourselves in agreement with God's purpose humbly takes the spotlight off of our own opinion and shines it toward His glory, which we were created for. (Isaiah 43:7)

MARY'S SELF-TALK SONG

You can imagine the negative things other people said about Mary, mother of Jesus, as a pregnant unwed teenager. Her mind may have tried to run amok as she considered what others thought of her, but her encounter with the Holy Spirit converted her self-talk. Her thoughts overflowed in a praise song to God in which she proclaims, "from now on all generations will call me blessed, for the Mighty One has done great things for me." (Luke 1:48,49) It's time to call yourself blessed! There's a song of praise in you that will transform your self-talk in agreement with God's promises over you. Stop the sabotage and verbal abuse. God has a new song for your upgraded sound system!

CHALLENGE:

⇒ Find a mirror. Read Psalm 139 out loud over yourself as you look into it.

⇒ Write out a personal letter to the Father thanking Him for how he uniquely made you.

RETHINK:

⇒ Keep an inventory of your self-talk. Note the tone. Would you talk to someone you love the way you speak to yourself?

⇒ What negative things are stuck on repeat in your mind? Write out God's promises and replace that recording with a positive one about yourself.

⇒ Do you argue with other people in your mind? How would they respond if they could see your thought bubbles? Pray about adjusting your self-talk towards others.

⇒ Talk with a mentor or pastor about God's beautiful "built-ins" (gifts and callings) uniquely designed in you.

⇒ Find yourself in God's Word! Read the "I Am Promises" in the Appendix, study them and say them over yourself.

RENOVATING PRAYER:

Father, I repent for the hateful and negative things I've said to myself. I see how they dishonor you and discredit your creation. I am your workmanship. There is beauty and brilliance in me because I'm made in your image! Change my self-talk to honor you. Help me find myself in Your Word. Show me how you see me. Holy Spirit, help me discover my strengths and spiritual gifts so I can bring glory to God and advance His Kingdom as a faithful steward. In Your mighty name I pray, amen.

 ARTISTRY: *What beautiful thought is the Holy Spirit inspiring in the décor of your mind? How does He see you?*

DAY 18: WALLPAPER WORRY

RENOVATING THOUGHT: TURN WORRY INTO WORSHIP AND LET YOUR MIND WANDER INTO THE FOG (FAVOR OF GOD)!

Don't worry about anything; instead, pray about everything. Tell God what you need, and thank him for all he has done. Then you will experience God's peace, which exceeds anything we can understand. His peace will guard your hearts and minds as you live in Christ Jesus.
—*Philippians 4:6-7 (NLT)*

One of the most anticipated aspects of renovations is making style, color scheme and accessory choices. I'm very well acquainted with the Sherwin Williams color wheel sample block. When renovating our newly acquired church building, we picked a spectrum strip of dark to light greys—Black Fox to Reposed Gray. All design decisions had to line up with this palette, or they would clash with inconsistency and confusion. What standards of style, color and pattern will you use in your mind renovation?

PEACE IS THE STANDARD

As we explore the decor of our thought reno, let's aim to make peace our style standard. Everything must coordinate with it, or it's out!

... and the peace of God, which surpasses all understanding, will guard your hearts and minds through Christ Jesus. — Philippians 4:7 (NKJV)

There will be all kinds of people forcing their opinions about how you should decorate the newly renovated walls of your mind, but imagine there's a guard at the door asking, *"Does it match with peace?"* Philippians 4 lists the accessories that coordinate with this standard:

Finally, brothers and sisters, whatever is true, whatever is noble, whatever is right, whatever is pure, whatever is lovely, whatever is admirable—if anything is excellent or praiseworthy—think about such things. — Philippians 4:8 (NIV)

These things are our inspirational focus board. It's important to keep them in front of us because the devil is going to try to wallpaper the walls with worry!

You may be asking, "If we're only supposed to think about the good stuff, what about the bad stuff? We can't just stick our head in the sand, right?" Notice the Bible tells us to meditate on the high things listed in Philippians 4. Yes, we have to address the "not so lovely things" too, but they are not the focus of our thoughts.

We acknowledge, confront and deal with negative feelings or issues. Negative thoughts are sorted and evicted, but positive ones get to hang their pictures on the wall.

WHERE DOES YOUR MIND WANDER?

Like hopping from stone to stone in a raging river of nervous "what ifs," our mind chases rabbits of worry. Joyce Meyer says, "Worry is like a rocking chair, always in motion, but never getting you anywhere." [1]

In Old English, the root word for "worry" is *wyrgan*, which means, "to strangle or choke, like a dog gnaws and tears at a bone." [2] Isn't this how worry makes you feel in the pit of your stomach? It gnaws and tears at you.

Jesus commands us not to worry. (Matthew 6:25) He tells us to "let not" our hearts be troubled. (John 14:27) Jesus' directives are for our emotional and physical health. Doctors agree that chronic worry deteriorates our health in multiple ways, including ulcers, digestive problems, hormone imbalances, suppression of immune system and premature artery disease.

TURN WORRY INTO WORSHIP

If your mind often wanders to worry, congratulations! You're all set to learn to worship. Worry is ruminating on the potential ruin; worship is pondering on the promise!

If you can worry, you can worship.

Worry's finger points toward panic, shouting, "Hurry, faster...follow me this way!" After traipsing through paths of uncertainty and clouds of confusion, you look around frantically to realize you're lost and alone in a brain fog of hopelessness. When we worry we torment ourselves; we do the devil's job for him.

Worry does not empty tomorrow of its sorrow, it empties today of its strength. —Corrie Ten Boom

On the other hand, worship directs us toward the One who holds the compass of life. As we surrender our frets and fears to His promise, we find ourselves surrounded by His steadfast strength. In worship we realize we are not alone. As His presence fills the cavities of despair with renewed hope, our brain fog turns into a glory FOG—the FAVOR OF GOD!

I KNOW THAT

Ralph Hagemeier is an amazing man of God and lifelong missionary to the Democratic Republic of Congo. Over 25 years ago he preached a message that still resonates in my mind. In his message, Ralph encouraged us that...

We may not know HOW...
How will it all work out and be okay?
We may not know WHEN...
Oh, Lord, when will You deliver me from this?
We may not know WHERE...
Where will the provision come from?
We may not even know WHY...
Why is this happening, Lord? I don't understand.
But, we can know THAT!

> *I will praise you, for am fearfully and wonderfully made; Marvelous are Your works, And **THAT** my soul knows very well.*
> *— Psalm 139:14 (NKJV, emphasis added)*

I know THAT. He loves me and made me for a purpose. I am His, and *that I know well.* Life is a mystery, and we may never know the how, when, where, and why—but peace comes in knowing *that!*

THINGS DON'T HAVE TO BE PERFECT TO HAVE PERFECT PEACE

As a pastor, worry is a major battle for me. I really love the people in my care, and if they are hurting, it's so hard for me not to worry. For years I would have trouble sleeping and anxiously wake up ruminating over someone's problem. One night I felt the Lord say, "Kris, go ahead and be happy now."

I replied, "What, Lord? I can't. There are just so many issues and tragedies!"

His peace washed over me as I felt Him say, "If you're reaching people, there will always be a problem. There will always be a reason to be upset, but there are many more to thank ME for. Stop waiting for everything to be perfect before you have peace because life will pass you by with regret."

You will keep him in perfect peace, Whose mind is stayed on You, Because he trusts in You. — Isaiah 26:3 (NKJV)

I'm not perfect yet, but I'm making progress. I still wake up in the middle of the night with individuals on my heart, but instead of worrying, I pray and worship Him for the answer. Worry wastes your time; prayer produces breakthrough. Peace is yours now, here in the struggle. *Shalom.* It is the peace of God that doesn't make sense to your mind, but soothes your soul. Will you receive it? Just go ahead and be happy.

RETHINK:

⟹ Recollect your thoughts from yesterday. Which ones are on the design list in Philippians 4:8?

⟹ What are some ways you can place boundaries in your life to help peace protect your mind? (Ex. When my husband is traveling, I never watch shows about plane crashes or loved ones tragically dying because it can invite fear and worry.)

⟹ In your journal jot down the top five things you're worried about. Can you do anything about them? Say a prayer and see if the Holy Spirit gives you any specific action steps. If not, draw a box around them and write, "I trust these to you, Lord."

RENOVATING PRAYER:

Lord, help me choose to worship instead of worry. I pray for the Holy Spirit to set an alarm off when my mind begins to wander into worry. Help me to flip worry into worship! I trust that you love me and are faithful to complete what you've started. As I put my hope in you, help me to walk in the FOG—the favor of God. I receive your favor into every uncertain circumstance in my life. Your Kingdom come and your will be done in Jesus name!

ARTISTRY: *What beautiful thought is the Holy Spirit inspiring in the décor of your mind?*

DAY 19: INSPIRED IMAGINATION

RENOVATING THOUGHT: MY MIND IS A THINK TANK FOR GOD'S CREATIVE IDEAS AND DREAMS.

Now to him who is able to do immeasurably more than all we ask or imagine, according to his power that is at work within us.
—Ephesians 3:20 (NIV)

One of the Father's favorite questions is, "What do you see?" He created a divine process of seeing before being. Before we see it in the natural, God wants us to see it in the spirit. Abraham saw stars. Moses saw freedom. Isaiah saw a train in the temple. Jeremiah saw the branch. Elijah saw rain. Ezekiel saw an army. Joel saw an outpouring. Mary saw a Messiah.

All of these visions were seen in the "mind's eye" (a mental image / idea from the Holy Spirit) before they happened in the natural.

Now faith is the turning of dreams into deeds; it is betting your life on the unseen realities. -Hebrews 11:1 (Cotton Patch Gospel Version) [1]

Your mind remodel has an unprecedented purpose. God is creating a studio where your imagination can roam free beyond manmade limits. You can start sketching the visions the Holy Spirit reveals to you and write down the dreams He's sparking for your future. It all begins with the dream seed.

DREAM LIKE YOUR DAD

In the beginning God dreamed of a family, pondered how He would fashion one, and then created them with the seed of His word.

First this: God created the Heavens and Earth—all you see, all you don't see. Earth was a soup of nothingness, a bottomless emptiness, an inky blackness. God's Spirit brooded like a bird above the watery abyss.
— *Genesis 1:1-2 (The Message)*

The Hebrew word *yatsar* is used to describe this process of creation. It means, "to fashion, create or imagine." The power to create begins with the ability to dream! You may be thinking, "Okay, but I'm not creative." ***How could someone made in the CREATOR'S image not be creative?*** It's your inheritance; it's the mind of Christ. You are a creative being whether you realize it or not.

To "create" means to make or bring into existence something new. God is the master at creating something new out of "the soup of nothingness." He created our imaginations to do the same thing: to create wealth (Deuteronomy 8:18), to create solutions to society's problems and to create ways to reach people with the Gospel. God created our brilliant minds to see or imagine something out of nothing. That's called faith!

And without faith it is impossible to please God, because anyone who comes to him must believe that he exists and that he rewards those who earnestly seek him. — *Hebrews 11:6 (NIV)*

Do you need a solution to a problem? *Imagine!* Do you need a breakthrough with a new job? *Imagine* how God wants to bless you. Do you struggle with insecurity in relationships? *Imagine* how He is healing you. Jesus told us to receive the Kingdom with the faith of a child. That faith is the kind that doesn't have any problem sitting on Jesus' lap, laughing and imagining His purposes over us.

"... that is, God who gives life to the dead and calls into being that which does not exist. — Romans 4:17 (AMP)

The woman with the issue of blood *imagined* her healing. If she could just touch the hem of Jesus' robe, virtue would reach her (Luke 8:43-48. She dreamed it; then she spoke it. She received a creative miracle from Jesus with creative, childlike faith!

CREATIVE ANOINTING

I believe God is stirring up a creative anointing to touch all the "Seven Mountains of Culture" (Religion / Family / Business / Education / Government / Arts & Entertainment / Media) for His glory. Yes, musicians and artists are creative, but so are mathematicians and engineers! It's easy to appreciate Walt Disney types, but have you heard of Johannes Kepler? He was a Christian best known for discovering the three mathematical laws of planetary motion and the elliptical patterns in which the planets travel around the sun. When asked about his scientific advancements he said, *"I think God's thoughts after him"* [2]

No matter your personality, you are creative if you think God's thoughts! We are called to think like the Father and fill our thought life with imaginations of His goodness.

THINK OUTSIDE YOUR BOX

This anointing includes creative solutions! Countless times I've prayed, "Lord, I don't know how to fix this, show me how." And a fresh idea will come to mind. The Bible says in Jeremiah 33:3, "Call to Me, and I will answer you, and show you great and mighty things, which you do not know." Our minds are laboratories of discovery, studios of creativity and cafes of conversation connected with God's Kingdom purposes.

One God-inspired idea could change your life forever. Everything you see began with an idea or a dream. God dreams are designed to reach far beyond us and bless multiple people, generations and even nations!

Every thought we think is creating our future. — Louise Hay

RETHINK:

⇒ What did you dream of doing as a child? Can you see hints of God's destiny there?

⇒ Do you let yourself dream and imagine? Can you see yourself prospering and overcoming? Think of an area of challenge in your life. Take a few minutes to see yourself overcoming.

⇒ Let's learn from Joseph. Many times God plants dreams that are only for us to ponder for a season because other people can't handle it. Have you ever let other people steal your dream seed? Read Luke 2:19 about how Mary pondered things.

⇒ Read The Parable of the Seed in Matthew 13. What is the greatest threat to your dream seeds?

⇒ This week if you're faced with a challenge at work or home, pray for the Holy Spirit to give you a creative solution and be ready to receive fresh inspiration.

RENOVATING PRAYER:

Lord, thank You for making me creative like you. I pray that your power would work in me. I believe that you can do exceedingly, abundantly and beyond all I could ever ask or imagine. Stretch my mind like Abraham's to see what you're dreaming over my life. Make my heart fertile soil to sprout your big ideas. I ask you for a new creative anointing that touches every part of my life. Thank you for creative solutions and creative ideas. Make my mind a laboratory to imagine your goodness. In your powerful name, Jesus, I pray, amen.

 ARTISTRY: *What beautiful thought is the Holy Spirit inspiring in the décor of your mind?*

DAY 20: WASTED BRAIN CELLS

RENOVATING THOUGHT: DON'T WASTE BRAIN CELLS ON THINGS THAT DON'T MATTER!

Therefore, since we are surrounded by such a great cloud of witnesses, let us throw off everything that hinders and the sin that so easily entangles. And let us run with perseverance the race marked out for us.
—Hebrews 12:1 (NIV)

One of my favorite responses to life's demands has become, "I'm not going to waste brain cells on that." I grew up with the famous anti-drug "Just Say No" slogan championed by Nancy Reagan. Remember the commercial featuring an egg in a sizzling skillet with a voice saying, "This is your brain ... this is your brain on drugs ... any questions?" I vowed to protect my brain cells from impending frying pans! I was armed and ready to avoid sniffing paint and cocaine, but there's another brain cell killer that threatens us every day. Stress.

Scientists have discovered that prolonged stress damages brain cells. Cortisol creates a surplus of the neurotransmitter glutamate. Glutamate creates free radicals, unattached oxygen molecules, that attack brain cells in the same way that oxygen attacks metal, causing it to rust. Stress makes your brain rust! In addition to damaging brain cells, prolonged stress can also affect blood pressure and fats in the blood increasing the risk of heart attack and stroke.[1]

I'm too blessed to be stressed.

SMART STRESS OR STUPID STRESS?

Here's the quandary: killing brain cells by taking drugs is avoidable, but avoiding all stress is impossible. Jesus even said we would have trouble in this world but should take heart; He has overcome the world. (John 16:33) Yep, we're all going to experience stress.

I like to divide stress into two categories: SMART stress and STUPID stress. Smart stress is pressure God uses to call out greatness in us. Just as God designed our natural bodies to react to "fight or flight" situations with a boost of hormones, He's enabled our spirits to rise up in the face of pressure with a boost of anointing! Tennis legend Billie Jean King said, "Pressure is a privilege." You're on the field, not the sideline. Like Esther, you've come to the Kingdom for such a time as this. (Esther 4:14) We only grow stronger when more weight is applied to our muscles—physically or spiritually. Every great leader was forged in the fire of great pressure.

But, there is also stupid stress. Stupid stress is stress we needlessly create that weighs us down and steals our brain energy. We can't control all the things life throws at us, but we can control what we throw at ourselves! Let's look at five things we should never waste our brain cells on.

5 THINGS TO NEVER WASTE BRAIN CELLS ON:

1. WHAT YOU CAN'T CHANGE

This is where the control freaks raise their hands and shout, "Oh, help me, Jesus!" Are you worrying about what you got on the test you took this morning? Do you keep thinking about how you could've pitched your business proposal better? Are you obsessing over the fluorescent color the neighbors are painting their house? What's the common denominator? These are all thing you can't change! You're wasting energy and creating stress worrying over what's already happened and can't be changed. You can learn and improve next time, but let go of the mistakes of the past.

If you can't change it, there is no grace in trying. If you can change it, God will show you the part you're responsible for; then trust Him with the rest.

If you don't like it change it; if you can't change it, change your attitude. —Maya Angelou

2. WHAT'S NONE OF YOUR BUSINESS

The Lord taught me a valuable lesson years ago. I was agonizing over a situation that I overheard my husband talking about on the phone as I eavesdropped through the cracked door. Stressed out, I moaned to the Lord saying, "Oh God, I can't stand the pain and pressure of this situation!" I felt the Lord show me I was actually never meant to deal with it. I wasn't even supposed to know about it, but I stuck my nose where it didn't belong. I did not have the grace to handle what I had learned because I had walked out of God's boundaries by being nosy. Stay in your place of grace!

You have enough stress dealing with what comes to you; don't go looking for trouble and stir up more stress and strife. Don't clutter your brain with the chatterbox of gossip. Remember, whatever stays in our mind must coordinate with Philippians 4:8.

3. WHAT OTHER PEOPLE THINK OF YOU

If we read a poll of your thoughts, how many would be deliberating over what people think of you? When we read the story of King Saul, we see that his thoughts of pleasing the people outweighed his thoughts toward

God. Pleasing people was King Saul's downfall, while David was a man after God's own heart. Leading our thoughts towards God's truth results in holy decisions that won't always be popular with people.

I consider myself to be a "recovering people pleaser," and this simple truth from Laurie Beth Jones' book *Jesus in Blue Jeans* is dear to my heart: "Some Will, Some Won't, So What, Someone's Waiting!" [2] We can't waste brain cells on what people are thinking about us. People are fickle, and if they think one thing today, they'll change it tomorrow. Continue to live out truth, and it will speak for itself.

4. THINKING EVIL OF OTHERS

Thinking negatively or evil of others sets toxins off in our brains that affect our whole bodies. Jesus said in Matthew 9:4, "Why do you entertain evil thoughts in your hearts?" (NIV) Our emotions follow the direction our thoughts determine. If you continue to focus on all the faults and negative qualities of someone, that's what they will be to you. The next time negative thoughts about someone try to eat your brain cells, turn it into a prayer for them.

> *...bless those who curse you, pray for those who mistreat you.*
> — *Luke 6:28 (NIV)*

5. WHAT STIRS UP STRIFE

There are so many arguments that do not matter! We can find arguments and disagreements on every conceivable issue on social media. Does that means we need to engage in each one we have an opinion about? Just because you're invited to an argument, doesn't mean you need to attend! Even if you're right, the stress it produces is not worth the fight. Pick battles that promote peace and that really matter. Ask yourself, "Does this affect eternity in any way? Will I even care next year or next week?" Protect your brain cells from needless, stupid arguments. Don't poke the bear!

Without wood a fire goes out; without a gossip a quarrel dies down. As charcoal to embers and as wood to fire, so is a quarrelsome person for kindling strife. — Proverbs 26:20-22 (NIV)

Stop wasting brain cells on things that don't matter. Instead, save them for times of smart stress and productive pressure. Use your brain cells to rise up and "run your race" like Hebrews 12 says. The heroes of faith applaud our turn as we take our lap in history. Let's give them something to cheer about!

RETHINK:

⇒ How many things that upset you today will still matter a month from now?

⇒ How do you react to stress? (Hide under the covers or run ahead in your own strength?)

⇒ Read 2 Corinthians 12:9. How can you find God's strength in your stress and grow stronger?

⇒ How do you feel about the quote, "Pressure is a privilege"? Are there any comfort zones God's called you out of that you're scared to leave?

⇒ Which of the five things do you struggle with the most? What is an action step to prevent this stress? (Ex. Limiting social media, refusing gossip, etc.)

RENOVATING PRAYER

Father, thank you for my miraculous brain. I pray for your healing where stress has hurt by body. Help me to save my brain for what really matters. Give me a spirit of discernment to see when I waste my energy on pointless things like worry, gossip and strife. Give me the grace to change my attitude about the things that I can't change and control. I give my control to you, Lord. Show me the things that are entangling my race for your Kingdom and help me to throw them off and rise up in new strength. Thank you Lord, for your strength!

ARTISTRY: *What beautiful thought is the Holy Spirit inspiring in the décor of your mind?*

DAY 21: THINK LIKE A WINNER

RENOVATING THOUGHT: AS I RECEIVE GOD'S STRENGTH, I CAN DO EVERYTHING HE'S CALLED ME TO DO.

I can do all things through Christ who strengthens me.
—Philippians 4:13 (NIV)

Remember the classic children's story *The Little Engine That Could*? It's hard to nail down the original author of this story because it's thought to be a folk tale, but one version appeared in a Sunday School publication in 1906 under the title, "Thinking One Can."

> I think I can. I think I can. I think I can.
> —Little Engine That Could

My great grandmother read me this story of optimism and would say, "'Can't' never could do anything!" Maybe you have failed in the past, but as Zig Ziglar said, *"Failing is an event, not a person. Yesterday ended last night."* There is more in you than yesterday's mistakes! Every failure is an opportunity to learn and try again;

it's not who you are! You're more than an overcomer in Christ! (Romans 8:37)

> You are what you think. So just think big, believe big, act big, work big, give big, forgive big, laugh big, love big and live big. —Andrew Carnegie

GOD THINKS YOU CAN

I love the story of Gideon because I can totally relate to it. Self-assurance and confidence were not featured on his resume. In Judges 6, we see Gideon "threshing wheat in the winepress" afraid of being attacked by the Midianites, who were terrorizing Israel. Threshing wheat usually takes place in a wide-open space, but Gideon was thinking small in a small place. Then the Angel of the Lord came to chat with Gideon under the oak tree.

> *The angel of the Lord came and sat down under the oak in Ophrah that belonged to Joash the Abiezrite, where his son Gideon was threshing wheat in a winepress to keep it from the Midianites. When the angel of the Lord appeared to Gideon, he said, "The Lord is with you, mighty warrior."*
> *— Judges 6:11-12 (NIV)*

We would look at Gideon and see a cowardly little man hiding in a winepress hoping not to draw attention, but God's thoughts were beyond those facts. God saw a mighty warrior! Gideon lacked the "Little Engine's" enthusiasm. He didn't "think he could" and went on to argue with an angel!

Gideon's Thoughts:

Why has all this happened to us?
My clan is the weakest.
I'm the weakest in my family.
The Midianites are too mean and mighty!

God's Thoughts:

Gideon, you are a mighty warrior.
My presence is greater than the enemy.
I'm answering the cry of my people and showing my glory.
I will go with you.

God met Gideon's negative thoughts with thoughts of His purpose to deliver His people. Negative thoughts aren't ignored and swept under the rug; they are addressed with truth. Gideon was right. The facts were that he was the smallest and the most insignificant, but the TRUTH was God was with him! The truth was God would use Gideon's weakness for His glory.

A negative thinker sees a difficulty in every opportunity. A positive thinker sees an opportunity in every difficulty. —Author Unknown

We all have facts looming in our circumstances that try to steal the truth. We want an "easy button" to life. But for God to show off His glorious grace, He needs some situations to overcome! In 2 Corinthians 2:14, Paul describes God: "...who always leads us in triumph in Christ..." Through the blood of Jesus, God is actively leading us into victory, not doubt and defeat. *The question is...are we following?* The first step to this victory parade begins in *following* HIS THOUGHTS!

> When you accept the fact that your true identity includes being an overcomer, you will never settle for less than a miracle. [1]
> —Craig Groeschel

COUNT THE TROPHIES

Are you counting the reasons *you can't*, or are you counting how *you CAN* with God's help? Let's stop and take a look at the new "trophies" that adorn your renovated mind mansion. They are glorious, but not as a memento to your own strength and agility but rather as glorious objects of God's overcoming grace. What are these trophies? They are testimonies hung in the corners of our minds. They stir up faith as we remember the wondrous things God has done before. Memories of His provision. Stories of answered prayers. Miracles in the midnight hour! Whenever you struggle to think victorious thoughts for your future, rehearse His Word, pull down the testimony trophies and remind yourself of all the times God has been faithful.

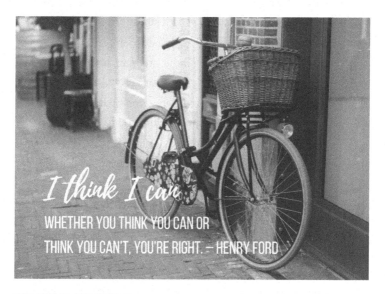

WE HAVE A WINNER

It's time to *make up your mind!* Will you agree with God's truth or continue to argue and count your excuses to fail? Only you can have the power to decide. Your decision is your destiny. I pray you choose life. You *can* do all things through Christ who gives you the strength! Those things He has called and anointed you to do. Don't underestimate the treasure in your clay. (2 Corinthians 4:7) We may not be enough in our own strength, but it's okay because our Father is calleßd, I Am.

Whether you think you can or think you can't, you're right. — Henry Ford

RETHINK:

⇒ Think through stories from the Bible. Write down ways you see God thinking like a winner in each story.

⇒ Write down at least five testimonies of God's goodness or deliverance in your life. (These are your testimony trophies! Collect these trophies and store them in your thoughts.)

⇒ What lie threatens your confidence and makes you think YOU are a failure rather than an overcomer who simply failed at an obstacle?

⇒ What things has God called you to that you have quit out of a mindset of defeat?

⇒ Journal about the difference in a mindset of defeat versus victory.

RENOVATING PRAYER:

Thank you Lord, for the renovation you've done in my mind. I pray you would put a "can do" spirit within me. Instead of counting the facts, help me to count by faith and embrace the truth. Download your thoughts and purposes for me into my mind. Help me to testify of your greatness and rehearse your goodness in my mind. I CAN DO all things through Christ who increases supernatural strength in me. Let your treasure shine out of this earthen vessel and amaze all who witness it with your goodness and glory! Your victory is my triumph. In the victorious name of Jesus, amen.

 ARTISTRY: *What beautiful thought is the Holy Spirit inspiring in the décor of your mind?*

NOTES

Day 1

1. Vanitzian, Donie. "It's Hard to Believe but a Condo Could Be Lost to Squatters." Los Angeles Times, 15 July 2017, www.latimes.com/business/la-fi-associations-squatters-20170715-story.html.

2. Rowe, Tim. *Heart: The Key To Everything In The Christian Life.* Lulu Publishing Services, 2016.

Day 2

1. Dougherty, Elizabeth. "What Are Thoughts Made Of?" 26 April, 2011, www.engineering.mit.edu/engage/ask-an-engineer/what-are-thoughts-made-of/.

2. Leaf, Dr. Caroline. "You Are What You Think: 75-98% of Mental and Physical Illnesses Come from Our Thought Life!" 11 Nov. 2011, www.drleaf.com/blog/you-are-what-you-think-75-98-of-mental-and-physical-illnesses-come-from-our-thought-life/.

3. Ascoli, Giorgio A. "Trees of the Brain, Roots of the Mind." MIT Press, 9 Apr. 2015, www.mitpress.mit.edu/books/trees-brain-roots-mind.

4. Thayer, Joseph H. *Thayer's Greek - English Lexicon of the New Testament.* Baker Book House.

Day 3

1. Strong, James. *Strong's Exhaustive Concordance of the Bible.* Hendrickson Pub., 2012.

2. White, Duane. *Huperman,* Beyond These Shores, 2006.

3. Strong, James. *Strong's Exhaustive Concordance of the Bible.* Hendrickson Pub., 2012.

4. Strong, James. *Strong's Exhaustive Concordance of the Bible.* Hendrickson Pub., 2012.

5. Strong, James. *Strong's Exhaustive Concordance of the Bible.* Hendrickson Pub., 2012.

6. Rowe, Tim. *Heart: The Key To Everything In The Christian Life.* Lulu Publishing Services, 2016.

Day 5

1. Irving L. Jensen, *How to Profit From Reading the Bible,* Moody Press, Chicago, 1985, p. ix.

Day 6

1. Covey, Stephen R. The 7 Habits of Highly Effective People: Signature Program: Achieving Personal and Interpersonal Effectiveness from the inside Out. Franklin Covey, 2005.

Day 7

1. Vallotton, Kris (kvministries). "If you embrace the promise without the process, you are living in a fantasy." 29 September 2016, 8:02 PM. Tweet.

2. Zimmerman, Alan R. *Pivot: How One Turn in Attitude Can Lead to Success.* Peak Performance Publishers, 2006.

PHASE 2:

1. Hunt, T. W. *Mind of Christ: the Transforming Power of Thinking His Thoughts.* Broadman, Holman, 1997.

Day 8

1. Strong, James. *Strong's Exhaustive Concordance of the Bible.* Hendrickson Pub., 2012.

Day 9

1. Powlison, David. "Sanctification is a Direction." Crossway. Crossway USA. 16 August 2017, https://www.crossway.org/articles/sanctification-is-a-direction/

Day 10

1. "The Art of 'Quotemanship' and 'Misquotemanship.'" The Art of Quotemanship and Misquotemanship, blogs.umb.edu/quoteunquote/2012/05/08/its-a-much-more-effective-quotation-to-attribute-it-to-aristotle-rather-than-to-will-durant/.

2. White, Kris. *Huperwoman,* Beyond These Shores, 2010.

3. Duhigg, Charles. *The Power of Habit: Why We Do What We Do in Life and Business. Random House Inc,* 2014.

Day 11

    1. Thoreau, Henry David. *Walden.*

    2. "Donald Hebb Formulates the 'Hebb Synapse' in Neuropsychological Theory (1949)." Donald Hebb Formulates the "Hebb Synapse" in Neuropsychological Theory (1949): HistoryofInformation.com,www.historyofinformation.com/expanded.php?id=4361.

    3. Lewis, C. S., et al. *Mere Christianity; a Revised and Enlarged Ed., with a New Introduction, of the Three Books: The Case for Christianity, Christian Behaviour and Beyond Personality.* Macmillan, 1971.

Day 12

    1. Giaimo, Cara. "Remembering the Victims of the Brooklyn Bridge Elephant Stampede." Atlas Obscura, Atlas Obscura, 4 Oct. 2017, www.atlasobscura.com/articles/staten-island-octopus-brooklyn-bridge-elephants-hoax-memorials.

    2. Staff, PT. "Stats on Panic Disorder." *Psychology Today,* Sussex Publishers, 1 July 1993, www.psychologytoday.com/articles/199307/stats-panic-disorder.

Day 13

    1. Tregelles, Samuel P. *Gesenius' Hebrew-Chaldee Lexicon.* Eerdmans, 1964.

    2. Leaf, Caroline. *Who Switched off My Brain?: Controlling Toxic Thoughts and Emotions. Inprov, Ltd.,* 2009.

Day 14

    1. White, Kris. *Huperwoman,* Beyond These Shores, 2010.

    2. *Life Application Study Bible.* Tyndale House Publishers, Incorporated, 2011.

Day 15

    1. Brown Brené. *Daring Greatly: How the Courage to Be Vulnerable Transforms the Way We Live, Love, Parent and Lead.* Avery, 2015.

2. "Want an Abundant Life? Change Your Thinking." Michael Hyatt, 26 July 2017, michaelhyatt.com/change-your-thinking/.

Day 16

1. "Negativity Bias." Wikipedia, Wikimedia Foundation, 12 Jan. 2018, en.wikipedia.org/wiki/Negativity_bias

2. Hanson, Ph.D. Rick. "Confronting the Negativity Bias." *The Huffington Post*, TheHuffingtonPost.com, 8 Oct. 2010, www.huffingtonpost.com/rick-hanson-phd/be-mindful-not-intimidate_b_753646.html.

3. Benson, Kyle. "The Magic Relationship Ratio, According to Science." The Gottman Institute, 4 Oct 2017, https://www.gottman.com/blog/the-magic-relationship-ratio-according-science/

4. Robson, David. "Future - The Contagious Thought That Could Kill You." BBC, BBC, 11 Feb. 2015, www.bbc.com/future/story/20150210-can-you-think-yourself-to-death.

Day 17

1. Warren, Richard. *The Purpose-Driven Life: What on Earth Am I Here for?* Zondervan, 2016. (Accredited to C.S. Lewis)

Day 18

1. "The Cause and Cure for Worry." *Joyce Meyer Ministries*, www.joycemeyer.org/everydayanswers/ea-teachings/the-cause-and-cure-for-worry.

2. "Worry." Merriam-Webster, *Merriam-Webster*, www.merriam-webster.com/dictionary/worry.

Day 19

1. Jordan, Clarence L. *Cotton Patch Version of the Epistles*. Koinonia Publications, 1964.

2. "Man of Science, Man of God: Johann Kepler." *The Institute for Creation Research*, www.icr.org/article/science-man-god-johann-kepler/.

Day 20

    1. "Stress: Your Brain and Body." Stress and the Brain. Ed. At-Bristol. Wellcome Trust, n.d. Web. 05 Mar. 2018.

    2. Jones, Laurie Beth. Jesus in Blue Jeans: a Practical Guide to Everyday Spirituality. MJF Books, 2009.

Day 21

    1. Groeschel, Craig. *Altar Ego: Becoming Who God Says You Are.* Christian Large Print, 2014.

APPENDIX

I AM PROMISES - GOD'S THOUGHTS OVER YOU

Replace negative thoughts with God's thoughts of truth. Here are just a few of God's abundant promises over you. Speak them out loud over yourself. Look up the scriptures and study them. Write out which ones speak to your negative thoughts and place them in a prominent space you'll see throughout the day.

I AM...

I am called of God - 2 Timothy 1:9

I am chosen - 1 Thessalonians 1:4

I am the apple of my Father's eye - Psalm 17:8

I am being changed into His image - 2 Corinthians 2:18

I am a new creation in Christ - 2 Corinthians 5:17

I am seated with Christ in heavenly realms - Ephesians 2:6

I am the temple of the Holy Spirit - 1 Corinthians 6:19

I am forgiven of all my sins - Ephesians 1:7

I am redeemed from the curse of the law - Galatians 3:13

I am blessed - Galatians 3:9

I am above and not beneath - Deuteronomy 28:13

I am loved and chosen - Colossians 3:12

I am victorious - Revelation 12:11

I am one in Christ - John 17:21

I am fearfully and wonderfully made - Psalm 139:14

I am set free - John 8:31

I am His workmanship - Ephesians 3:20

I am adopted as His child - John 1:12

I am a friend of God - John 15:15

I am complete in Christ - Colossians 2:10

I am assured that all things work together for good
- Romans 8:28

I am free forever from condemnation - Romans 8:1,2

I am bought with a price. I belong to Christ
- 1 Corinthians 6:20

I am born of God and the evil one cannot touch me
- 1 John 5:18

I am given eternal life - John 3:15

I am connected to the love of God and nothing can separate me
- Romans 8:35

I am more than a conqueror - Romans 8:37

I am a part of the body of Christ - 1 Corinthians 12:27

I am fully known - 1 Corinthians 13:12

I am guarded by peace - Philippians 4:7

I am the healed of the Lord - Isaiah 53:5, 3 John 2

I am redeemed from destruction and crowned with loving-
kindness - Psalm 103:4

DAILY MIND RENEWAL DECLARATION:
Direct your "Train of Thought" with the God's Promises

Just as Jesus stood with authority and spoke PEACE to the storm. (Mark 4:39) We have the authority in Christ to speak PEACE to our minds. We can take control of the runaway "thought train" derailing our destiny. As we pray and declare these truths, we transform our minds into the renewed "mind of Christ". (1 Cor. 2:16) Pray this declaration out loud. God's word is living and active. When your mind hears you speak the Word, there's a connection that solidifies the transformation in your thoughts and stirs up your faith! Your words release heaven to act in your life. Don't be afraid to pray out loud. Your mind needs to hear how you're directing it. There's a BIG connection between your mind and your mouth—let it work for you, not against you!

PEACE OF MIND

I submit my mind, my thoughts and my whole heart to the Lordship of Jesus Christ. (Luke 10:27) Jesus rules my thoughts. I have the mind of Christ. I listen to the voice of my Father God and I choose to follow him—I will not follow another. (John 10:27) **I declare peace guards my mind. Like a security guard, peace decides which thoughts can remain and which must go.** (Phil. 4:7) Peace rules over my mind. My mind is not like a runaway train. I take command and direct my mind into God's good plan and purpose. (Jer. 29:11) I speak peace to every racing anxious thought. Peace to panic. Just as Jesus spoke peace to the storm, I speak PEACE to the storm in my mind. Be still. I speak peace to any troubled thoughts. I take authority in Jesus' name over fear, worry and anxiety. Psalm 23 says, He leads me by still waters and restores my soul. (Ps. 23: 2) My soul - my mind, will and emotions are being restored, renewed and transformed by His power. I receive peace now. His perfect peace pushes out every anxious thought. Perfect peace casts out fear. (1 John 4:18) Christ's abundant love decorates the walls of my mind and evicts fear and anxiety.

SOUND MIND WITH UNLIMITED POSSIBILITIES

God's not given me a spirit of fear, but power, love and a sound mind. (2 Tim. 1:7) I declare I have a sound mind. Every thought must come into alignment with the Word of God. Today I set my mind on things above (Col.3: 2), and my attitude is being renewed (Ephesians 4:23). I'm not stuck on yesterday. I will not obsess on my weakness and failure, but I fix my attention on God's power that works in me to overcome! (1 John 4:4) I receive fresh vision, a new mentality—from glory to glory, strength to strength, faith to faith—my mind is renewed! **My mind is framed with the limitless possibilities of my Father—not by the limits of my feelings, my failures and my frustration.** I fix my thoughts in agreement with God's goodness and abundance over me. I walk in the F.O.G.—the favor of God and it starts with thinking favorable thoughts. I choose to think on things that are true, honest, just, pure, lovely and of good report. (Phil. 4:8)

PRODUCTIVE MIND

My mind is a laboratory of discovery, a studio of creativity and a cafe of conversation connected with God's Kingdom purposes. I have an open and responsive mind to God's Spirit and Word. I receive His creative solutions, His divine revelations and His "aha" moments. God designed my mind with a purpose. He wired my mind and my personality to worship Him. I will use my thoughts to love and serve Him. My mind is filled with light and clarity. I rebuke confusion, negativity, poverty and doubt. I am a child of God and I have a beautiful, fruitful and blessed mind. I am who God says I am. I tear down any stronghold or lie that tries to exalt itself above the knowledge of Christ. I declare today my mind is a channel of heaven receiving creative ideas, witty inventions and ingenious solutions to problems. Every day I revel at the magnificence of my God and His renewable resources! His greatness blows my mind! Today I look for ways to bless Him with my thoughts and be a blessing to others.

ONE WITH HIM

Every room in my thought house belongs to Him, filled with the life and the power of the Holy Spirit. I will NOT conform to the world's thinking, but be transformed to think thoughts of God's truth. God's truth sets me free! Today I will hide His Word in my heart. It washes my mind and cleanses me from any evil or impure thoughts by the blood of Jesus. His Word shapes my opinion. I think the Father's thoughts towards people and love them like He does. I set my mind in agreement and unity with the Holy Spirit. I am never alone because I am connected to God's love and life in me. (1 Cor. 6:17) **Let my thought life be a continual conversation with heaven.** I declare I have a beautiful mind. I have the mind of Christ Jesus, my Lord.

TRY THE S.O.A.P.Y. STUDY

Many people tell me they struggle to read the Bible and apply it to their life. The SOAP Bible study method will help you personally connect and apply the wealth of God's Word to your life. I'm not sure who actually invented the method, but I've been teaching and using it for years. It's a great option for people of all ages. (Our youth started SOAPY journals and surprisingly enjoyed it last year.) Few things make my heart happier than people discovering a love for God's Word.

S –SCRIPTURE. I suggest taking the scripture from each day of the *Mind Renovation* and doing a SOAPY to it. Look up the scripture. Read the context of the verse. Write out the scripture by hand or type it. (I find there's more of a connection with my brain when I write it out with different colors.) Look up a few different translations and write out the differences. (There are many Bible sites online that will give you different translations and paraphrases.)

O – OBSERVE. Who is the audience and context of the verse? Circle the words that stick out to you. Look up the definition of those words. (Use a concordance to find the Greek or the Hebrew if you so desire.) What truth sticks out to you? What's the main idea of the verse?

A – APPLY. How does this verse apply to your life in this season? How does it affect your life, your relationships and your attitude?

P – PRAY. Write out a prayer to The Father about the verse. Do you need to repent? Do you need strength? Pray God's word back to Him. There is power in praying the Word!

Y – YES! (I added the Y myself. You won't see this when you research the method.) I like to add a Y for Yes, because it is your FAITH declaration. It's the THOUGHT you take away to displace the lie of the enemy. It's your victory statement of God's promise.

Studying God's Word will change your MIND. Give it a try.

ABOUT THE AUTHOR

Kris White was born in the west Texas windy city of Amarillo. From her tire swing on the family farm, she prayed and dreamed that God would use her in a special way to touch the world. In 1991 she married Duane White and has served with him in various ministries for the last 27 years, including founding a missions network called Beyond These Shores. She is an international speaker who has ministered in over 25 nations and served as a missionary in the U.K. She has a Master of Ministry degree in Leadership from Southwestern Christian University in Bethany, Oklahoma. In 2007, she and her husband planted The Bridge Church in Denton, Texas (findthebridge.com). Kris is the mother of adult children, Kelsey, Cody and Ashton, and her Olde English Bulldog named Winston. She loves coffee, dance parties in the kitchen and watching for red birds. You can visit her blog at beyondkris.com.